NELSON KEY GEOGRAPHY

Foundations
Teacher's Handbook

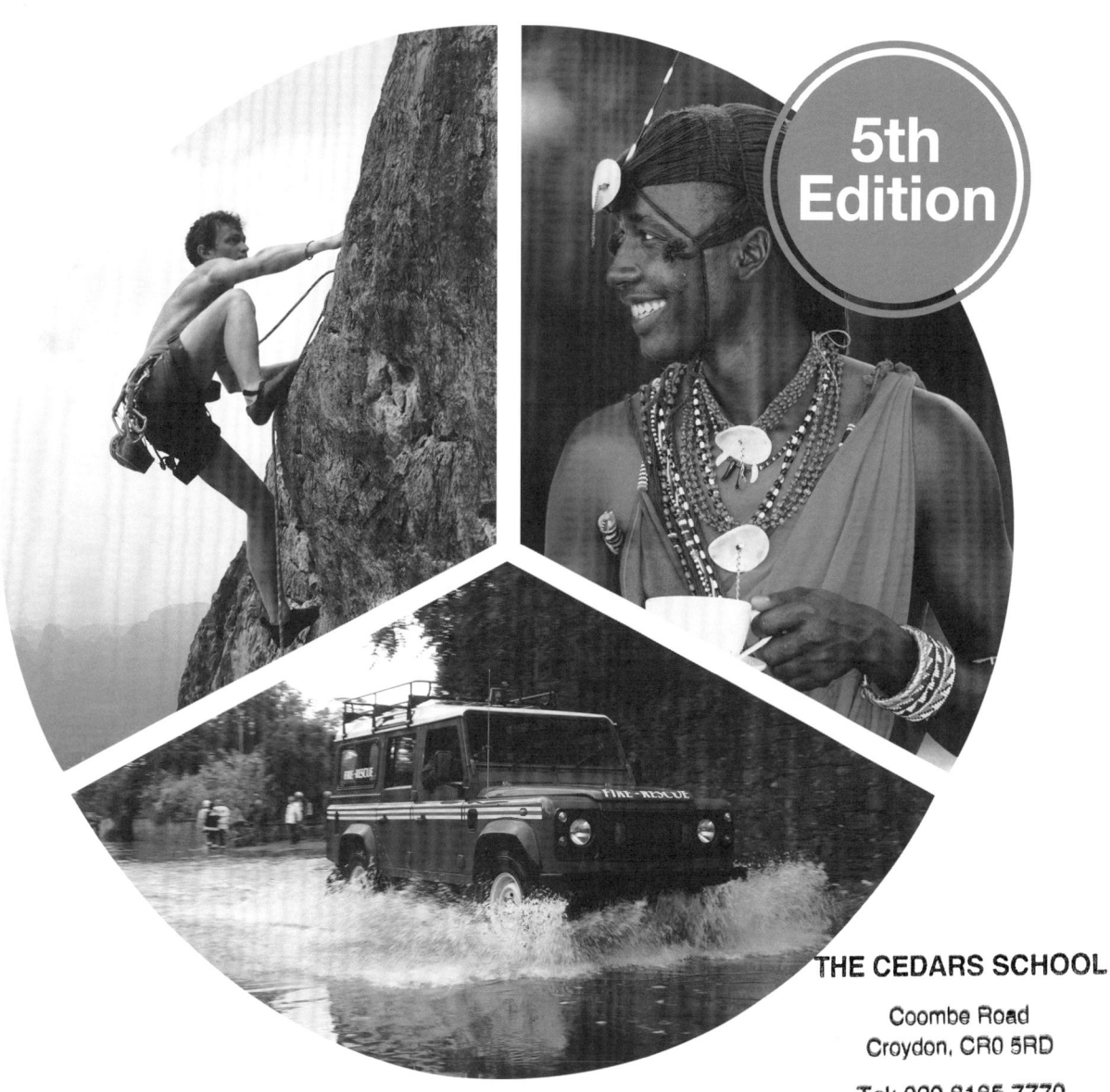

5th Edition

CATHERINE HURST AND NICHOLAS ROWLES

DAVID WAUGH AND TONY BUSHELL

OXFORD UNIVERSITY PRESS

OXFORD
UNIVERSITY PRESS

Great Clarendon Street, Oxford, OX2 6DP, United Kingdom

Oxford University Press is a department of the University of Oxford. It furthers the University's objective of excellence in research, scholarship, and education by publishing worldwide. Oxford is a registered trade mark of Oxford University Press in the UK and in certain other countries

© Oxford University Press 2014

Authors: Catherine Hurst and Nicholas Rowles

The moral rights of the authors have been asserted

First published in 2012

This edition 2014

All rights reserved. No part of this publication may be reproduced, stored in a retrieval system, or transmitted, in any form or by any means, without the prior permission in writing of Oxford University Press, or as expressly permitted by law, by licence or under terms agreed with the appropriate reprographics rights organization. Enquiries concerning reproduction outside the scope of the above should be sent to the Rights Department, Oxford University Press, at the address above.

You must not circulate this work in any other form and you must impose this same condition on any acquirer

British Library Cataloguing in Publication Data
Data available

978-1-40-852731-3

10 9 8 7 6 5 4 3 2 1

Paper used in the production of this book is a natural, recyclable product made from wood grown in sustainable forests.
The manufacturing process conforms to the environmental regulations of the country of origin.

Printed in Spain by Graphycems

Acknowledgements

The publishers would like to thank the following for permission to use photographs and other copyright material:

Illustrations by Kathy Baxendale, Nick Hawken, Angela Knowles, Gordon Lawson, GreenGate Publishing Services, Richard Morris, David Russell, Tim Smith, John Yorke

Cover photographs: Dudarev Mikhail/Shutterstock; Martin Harvey/Alamy; TA Crafts/iStockphoto

Every effort has been made to contact copyright holders of material reproduced in this book. Any omissions will be rectified in subsequent printings if notice is given to the publisher.

Links to third party websites are provided by Oxford in good faith and for information only. Oxford disclaims any responsibility for the materials contained in any third party website referenced in this work.

Contents

How to use this book — 5

1 What is geography?

What is physical geography? / What is human geography? — 6
What is environmental geography? — 8
How can we find where places are? — 9
How can we use graphs in geography? — 10
What is the value and use of geography? — 11

2 Weather and climate

How might you observe and record the weather? — 12
How can local features affect temperature and wind? — 13
What is Britain's weather? — 14
How does it rain? — 15
Forecasting the weather – anticyclones — 16
Forecasting the weather – depressions — 17
The weather enquiry — 19

3 River flooding

What causes a river to flood? — 21
Floods in the UK, 2012 — 22
How does the UK cope with floods? — 23
How can the risk of flooding be reduced? — 24
The river flooding enquiry — 25

4 Urbanisation

How were the sites for early settlement chosen? — 26
What different settlements patterns are there? — 27
How do settlements change with time? — 28
What are the benefits and problems of cash settlement growth? — 30
Why are there different land use patterns in towns? — 31
Why does land use in towns change? — 32
Where do we shop? — 33
How has shopping changed? — 34
Traffic in urban areas – why is it a problem? — 35
Traffic in urban areas – is there a solution — 36
Where should the by-pass go? — 37
The urbanisation enquiry — 38

5 Kenya and Africa

What are Africa's main physical features?	39
What are Africa's main human features?	40
What are Kenya's main features?	41
What are Kenya's main physical features?	42
Why is Kenya's population unevenly spread / Present-day movements of population	43
What is it like living in Nairobi?	44
What is the Maasai way of life?	45
What is a developing country?	46
The Kenya enquiry	47

6 Ordnance Survey maps

How can we show direction?	48
How can we measure distance?	49
What are grid references?	50
How do we use six-figure grid references?	51
How is height shown on a map?	52
How do contours show height and relief?	53

7 Key skills: writing and photos

How can we use key questions?	54
How can we describe places?	55
What are key words and key sentences?	56
How can we describe physical features on a photograph?	57
How can we use photographs to study settlements?	58
What do aerial photos show?	59
How can we use satellite photos?	60

Appendices

Appendix 1: The weather enquiry	61
Appendix 2: The river flooding enquiry	62
Appendix 3: The urbanisation enquiry	63
Appendix 4: The Kenya enquiry	64

How to use this book

This Teacher's Handbook has been written to accompany the *Nelson Key Geography Foundations* pupil book. It is intended to provide:

- full support for newly qualified teachers
- ideas for experienced, but busy, geography teachers
- ideas for experienced teachers who are not geographers.

Its aim is to provide succinct, at-a-glance information specifically to:

- help provide teachers plan and deliver high-quality geography lessons
- provide support, ideas, and suggestions for the use of additional resources
- explain the geographical content of each unit
- provide answers to the activities in the pupil book.

Where items are included here as suggestions, i.e. the Skills builders and Differentiation suggestions, they are intended to be just that. They are not meant to be prescriptive. You may want to use them as they stand, or they may spark off other, better, ideas that you can use.

1 What is geography?

Pupil Book pages 6–7

What is physical geography?
What is human geography?

About this spread

This spread will help pupils to understand what geography is – that it is the inter-relationship between the physical and human elements, which combine to give us the environment. It focuses specifically on what physical geography is – the study of the earth's natural features.

This spread also explains what human geography is – the study of where and how people live. It introduces pupils to the different elements that make up human geography – population, settlement, communications and economic activity.

Learning outcomes

By the end of this spread pupils should be able to:

- understand what physical geography is
- describe how the atmosphere affects us
- describe how landforms change
- understand what human geography is
- explain what quality of life is.

Key vocabulary

- physical geography
- atmosphere
- weather
- climate
- landforms
- human geography
- population
- settlement
- economic geography
- quality of life
- communications
- trade
- economic activity

Learning objectives

On this spread pupils should learn:

- what physical geography is
- that changes in the atmosphere give us our weather and climate
- what landforms are
- that human geography covers the study of population, settlement, communications and economic activity
- what quality of life is.

Skills builder

There is a lot of subject-specific terminology in geography that some pupils might find difficult to grasp and remember. This spread introduces some of the key vocabulary to do with human geography – population, settlement, communications, economic activity and quality of life.

You can help pupils by displaying some of the subject-specific terminology around the classroom along with their definitions, and pupils can use the glossary at the back of the pupil book when they come across a term they need to look up.

Further discussion suggestions

- What would make you want to move from:
  - a your street
  - b your town
  - c your country?
- Why does Britain need a high-speed rail link like HS2 between London and the North?
- What is the difference between imports and exports, and how do they affect Britain's balance of trade?

1 What is geography?

Pupil Book pages 6–7

What is physical geography? What is human geography? (cont.)

Answers to activities

1 a and b

Physical geography		
Landforms	Weather	Vegetation
Beach	Atmosphere	Forest
Delta	Clouds	Grassland
Glacier	Rainfall	
Lake	Snow	
Limestone gorge	Thunderstorm	
Marsh	Wind	
Meander		
Ox-bow lake		
River		
Snow-covered mountain		
Spit		
Spur		
Stack		
Volcano		
Waterfall		
Wave-cut platform		

2 a Population geography is a study of the distribution of people over the earth's surface and the changes that are taking place. These changes may be in the size of the population or the movement of people between different places.

b Settlement geography is a study of where people live and how these places change over time.

c Economic geography is how people earn a living.

3 a, b and c

Human geography		
Population	Settlement	Economic
Reasons for places to be crowded	Problems in city centres	How rich people are
Why few people live in desert areas Traffic jams in city centres	The location of shopping centres	Looking for work
Immigrants moving into Britain	Traffic jams in city centres	Why the UK is richer than Kenya
Different beliefs and ways of life	Land use in a city	Car making industry

4 a 'Quality of life' is how happy or content people are with their lives and the environment where they live.

b Good quality of life:
- Good health
- Having a job
- Having enough money to go on holiday
- Living in an area free of crime
- Living in an area where there is plenty of open space and is not polluted
- Having plenty of friends and family

Poor quality of life:
- Living in a house without basic amenities, e.g. heating and lighting
- Living in an area where there is little security and in danger of suffering from crime
- Experiencing racial discrimination
- Not have a job which brings in a regular wage
- Suffering ill health
- An inability to read and write

1 What is geography?

Pupil Book pages 8–9

What is environmental geography?

About this spread

On this spread pupils learn that environmental geography is the combination of the physical (natural) environment of climate, landforms, soils and vegetation, and the human environment, which includes settlement and economic activities. They also learn that different environments need to be protected and managed.

Learning objectives

On this spread pupils should learn:

- what environmental geography is
- the difference between renewable and non-renewable resources
- that different environments need to be protected, managed and conserved.

Learning outcomes

By the end of this spread pupils should be able to:

- understand that environmental geography is the study of the surroundings in which people, plants and animals live
- describe the difference between renewable and non-renewable resources
- give an example of an environment that needs to be protected.

Key vocabulary

- environmental geography
- environment (physical and human)
- resources
- renewable resources
- non-renewable resources

Skills builder

Sometimes, pupils need help to find information. If you are asking them to conduct an internet research task, such as 'find out why some areas are protected as National Parks', try to direct them to a particular website (www.nationalparks.gov.uk).

Work through the task in a dummy run, if necessary. Choose your nearest park, then pupils should click on 'About us' and then scroll down until they come to the heading 'Not ours – but ours to look after'. The text below the heading includes two bullet points that explain the role of the National Parks.

Pupils can then click on the link to different National Parks on the left-hand side of the screen. They can then find any two reasons why the environment needs protection. For example, for the Exmoor National Park, they could range from the fact that wild ponies on Exmoor are rarer than giant pandas, to the fact that Exmoor's hedge banks (hedges grown on top of stone-faced or earth banks) are relatively rare, and define the landscape of the National Park and surrounding area.

Further discussion suggestions

- Is it true to say that Britain's entire environment has been altered by people's activities?
- What can you do to protect and conserve your environment?
- Where is your nearest National Park and what makes it special?

Answers to activities

1 a and b

Physical (natural) environment	Human environment
River	Town
Bay	Port
Headland	Holiday resort
Areas of scenic value	Pier

2 a Trees have been cut down; soil washed away; smoke is given off by factory; working quarry; dirty (polluted) river with dead fish; exhaust fumes from vehicles; dirty beach with sewage outlet; untreated sewage discharged into sea; oil slick on sea; buildings on farmland.

b Old quarry screened by trees; area protected as National Park; area protected as nature reserve.

1 What is geography?

Pupil Book pages 10–11

How can we find where places are?

About this spread

This spread looks at how we can find out where places are by using a globe or an atlas. Pupils are introduced to latitude and longitude (imaginary lines), which are used to locate places. Pupils are shown how to use latitude and longitude – lines of latitude go across the map, lines of longitude go up and down the map.

Learning outcomes

By the end of this spread pupils should be able to:
- understand that maps help us to find out where places are
- use latitude and longitude to find places on maps and atlases.

Key vocabulary

- latitude
- longitude

Learning objectives

On this spread pupils should learn:
- that we use maps to find out where places are
- that we use latitude and longitude to find out where places are on maps.

Skills builder

Latitude and longitude are imaginary lines. Latitude is measured in degrees north or south of the equator and longitude is measured in degrees east or west of Greenwich Meridian.

Pupils need to be able to use latitude and longitude to either find places or give their precise location. This spread provides pupils with practice in using latitude and longitude, and an atlas, to locate places. The interactive activities on Kerboodle can help to embed this skill.

Further discussion suggestions

- What are the Tropic of Cancer and Tropic of Capricorn?
- If you stand at the North Pole, will the rest of the world be east, south or west?

Answers to activities

1.
   a Cairo
   b Cape Town
   c Madrid
   d São Paulo

2. Allow pupils a little leeway in the latitude and longitude for **a–f**.
   a 53°N 0°W
   b 8°N 3°E
   c 56°N 37°E
   d 36°S 59°W
   e 4°S 36°E
   f 15°S 47°W

3. Page numbers will depend on the atlas used. Latitude and longitude in the table below were taken from the online world atlas (www.worldatlas.com).

Place	Country	Page number	Latitude	Longitude
New York	USA		40° 42'N	74° 0'W
Tokyo	Japan		35° 41'N	139° 41'E
Sydney	Australia		33° 52'S	151° 12'E
Calcutta (Kolkata)	India		22° 34'N	88° 21'E

1 What is geography?

Pupil Book pages 12–13

How can we use graphs in geography?

About this spread

On this spread pupils are introduced to the use of four types of graph – bar graphs, line graphs, pie graphs and scatter graphs.

Pupils may have to draw these in maths, but in geography they have to understand what they show. This spread explains how, and when, each type of graph may be used.

Learning outcomes

By the end of this spread pupils should be able to:
- interpret four types of graphs (bar, line, pie and scatter)
- select appropriate graphs to show different data.

Key vocabulary
- graphs

Learning objectives

On this spread pupils should learn:
- that graphs are diagrams that show information in a clear and simple way
- how to analyse graphs.

Skills builder

Throughout their study of geography, pupils will need to be able to construct different types of graphs, label and annotate them, and interpret them. This spread introduces pupils to how and why we use graphs in geography, and the differentiation and homework suggestions in Kerboodle build on this. Posters of when and where to use different types of graphs (bar; divided bar; line; compound line; pie; scatter; pictograms; population pyramids) hung on the walls can be useful.

Further discussion suggestions

- Which types of graphs are best for showing:
  a growth
  b proportion
  c links between two kinds of data?
- Which type of graph can show a trend?
- How might a bar graph and line graph be combined to show two kinds of data?

Answers to activities

1. a May, June, July, August
   b Approximately 96 mm
2. a Approximately 800 000 000.
   b The graph suggests that population will continue to increase rapidly in the future.
3. a Winter
   b 55%
4. a 80 mm
   b A
5. a Line graph
   b Bar graph
   c Pie graph

1 What is geography?

Pupil Book pages 14–15

What is the value and use of geography?

About this spread

The aim of this spread is to show pupils that the knowledge and skills they learn while studying geography will help them in the future. Physical, human and environmental geography will help them to understand the world around them, and the events that happen in the world. The knowledge and skills they learn can open the door to a variety of different career opportunities in the future.

Learning outcomes

By the end of this spread pupils should be able to:
- describe how the knowledge and skills learned in geography will help them to understand the world
- give examples of how geography is of value and use to people.

Learning objectives

On this spread pupils should learn:
- that the knowledge and skills learned in geography will be useful to them in the future.

Skills builder

The box called 'Skills in geography' on page 15 of the pupil book lists some key geographical skills:
- reading and using maps
- interpreting and using graphs and statistics
- using photos
- carrying out enquiries
- using questions and enquiry skills to find things out
- using computers.

Some of these skills have been introduced in this first unit of the pupil book. These skills, along with many others, are developed throughout this book.

Further discussion suggestions

- What events in the news might be better understood if you have studied geography?
- How can knowledge of geography help you to plan a round-the-world trip?

Answers to activities

1 a

Physical	Human	Environmental	Skills
Lake District scenery	Migration and asylum seekers	Pollution of rivers	Planning walking routes
Local flooding in south-east England	Traffic problems in your local area	Global warming	Using computers in ICT
Indian Ocean earthquake and tsunami		Damaging wildlife habitats	

b Pupils should add another two topics of their own choice to each column in the table.

2 Pupils' responses will depend on their own point of view. They should aim to give at least six ways geography will help in their own lives.

3 Careers included in the text include jobs in travel, town planning, weather forecasting, mapping, journalism and the environment. Pupils should list at least ten careers or jobs.

2 Weather and climate

Pupil Book pages 18–19

How might you observe and record the weather?

About this spread

This spread will help pupils to understand what weather is, what elements make up the weather, and how the weather can be observed and recorded. The weather is free and easily accessible, so this is a perfect opportunity for pupils to do some fieldwork – collecting and processing their own data. It might be possible for pupils to observe and record the weather in each lesson for the duration of the unit and record the results as a classroom display.

Learning objectives

On this spread pupils should learn:

- what weather is
- about the different elements of weather
- how some elements of weather are measured and recorded.

Learning outcomes

By the end of this spread pupils should be able to:

- define the term 'weather'
- describe how some elements of weather are measured and recorded.

Key vocabulary

- weather
- meteorology
- temperature
- precipitation
- wind speed and direction
- Beaufort scale
- clouds
- visibility

Skills builder

Help pupils to learn how to describe the weather. Firstly, they need to identify the main elements of the weather (temperature, precipitation, wind, cloud type and cover, visibility and general weather). Then they need to choose key words to describe the weather conditions. They should be using words such as: hot, warm, cool, cold; sunny, cloudy, dull, overcast; calm, light breeze, gusty wind, gales, etc.

Show them a weather report from the TV, listen to an example from the radio or look at the BBC or Met Office websites. They can then construct sentences to describe the weather.

Further discussion suggestions

- What's the strangest/most unusual weather you've ever experienced?
- Why does the direction from which the wind blows have an important influence on our weather?

Answers to activities

1. Weather is the condition of the atmosphere over a short period of time. It is made up of different elements including temperature, precipitation, wind speed and direction, cloud type and cover, and visibility. It is about how hot, cold, wet, dry, windy, calm, cloudy or sunny it is.

2. a and b

   Weather features to be observed and recorded: Temperature, Precipitation, Visibility, Cloud cover, Wind speed, Cloud type, Wind direction

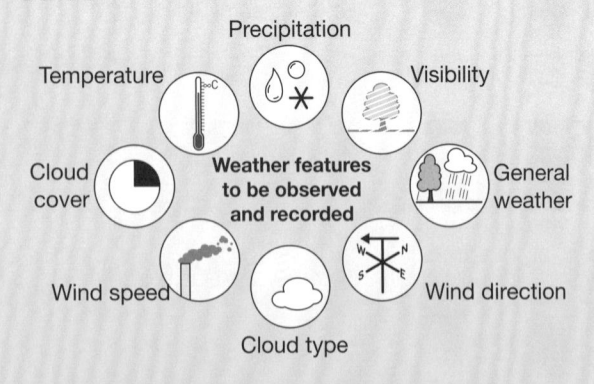

3.
   - Temperature is measured using a thermometer.
   - Wind direction is measured using a wind vane.
   - Wind strength is measured using the Beaufort scale.
   - Cloud cover is measured in eighths.

4. Pupils should sketch each of the cloud types in photos D. The descriptions linked to each cloud type are:
   - Cumulonimbus: huge towering clouds that often give showers.
   - Cumulus: dome shaped clouds with dark flat bases.
   - Stratus: low grey shapeless cloud that forms in layers.
   - Cirrus: high clouds that are wispy, light and featherlike.

5. a and b

   Pupils should record the weather in the same format as in table J.

6. a and b

   Pupils should record the weather for the week using the same format as in table J.

7. If the wind is coming from the west, the weather is likely to be cloudy with the likelihood of rain. It will be quite mild. If the wind is coming from the south, the temperatures will be quite high for the time of year. Winds from the east are likely to bring cold weather, especially in the winter. Northerly winds will keep the temperatures down and there is an increased chance of snow.

2 Weather and climate

Pupil Book pages 20–21

How can local features affect temperature and wind?

About this spread

This spread looks at how specific site conditions can affect the weather in a small area, such as around the school. Pupils will know there are differences, but they should be encouraged to think about what they are and what might cause them. They should recognise that our way of life and the environment both affects, and is affected by, weather and climate at a local scale.

Learning outcomes

By the end of this spread pupils should be able to:
- describe how site conditions, such as aspect, shelter, physical features and other factors can influence temperature, local wind speed and direction
- describe places at school that have different microclimates.

Key vocabulary

- microclimate
- aspect

Learning objectives

On this spread pupils should learn:
- that local features affect temperature and wind
- that places can have their own microclimates.

Skills builder

Using different types of photos and being able to label and annotate them is a core geographical skill. Provide pupils with an aerial photo of the school and ask them to label it with the features that affect the school's microclimate. For more information on using aerial photos and what they show, see *Nelson Key Geography Foundations*, pages 110–117.

Further discussion suggestions

- Where is the windiest spot in your school grounds? Why is it so windy?
- How do aspect and shade affect temperatures in your school grounds?
- Why does steam rise from a tarmac road when the sun appears after a period of rain?

Answers to activities

1 a, b and c
Responses will depend on your individual school.

2

Local weather conditions:
- **Aspect** — Direction in which a place is facing
- **Surface** — Dark surfaces warm up most
- **Microclimate** — Climate conditions of a small area
- **Buildings** — Give off heat and warm surroundings
- **Shelter** — Reduces the effect of wind
- **Physical features** — Can affect both temperature and wind

3 *Aspect*
Hotter classrooms on sunny side of school.
Cooler classrooms due to shade and effect of wind.
Cool and windy in shade and facing wind.

Shelter
Play area sheltered from wind.
Cool in trees with less wind.

Others
Play area warmed by dark tarmac surface.
Some warmth from building.
Cool around edge of lake.

4 a and b

The results will depend on the layout of the school, the time of day, the season the year and the weather conditions at the time that the temperature readings were taken. The following results were taken in September and December.

	Time	North facing	South facing	Weather conditions
December	9 a.m.	−3 °C	−2 °C	Clear, cold and frosty
	Midday	0 °C	3 °C	Clear and sunny
	3 p.m.	1 °C	3 °C	Clear and sunny
June	9 a.m.	10 °C	12 °C	Raining
	Midday	8 °C	15 °C	Windy and cloudy
	3 p.m.	8 °C	17 °C	Sun with some cloud
	Average	4 °C	8 °C	

c The north-facing side of the school was colder than the south. The temperature went up from 9 a.m. reaching its highest at 3 p.m. It was warmer in June, even though it was cloudy compared with the clear conditions in December.

d The north-facing side was facing away from the sun and was therefore in shade. The sun was low in the sky in December and therefore, even though it was clear, the temperatures did not rise very much, especially on the north side. In June the effect of the sun on the temperature was most marked on the south-facing side in the afternoon.

2 Weather and climate

Pupil Book pages 22–23

What is Britain's weather?

About this spread

This spread defines climate and describes the main differences in temperature and rainfall across Britain. Temperatures decrease northwards in summer and eastwards in winter. This is because the sun has a greater effect in the south than the north in summer, while the North Atlantic Drift raises winter temperatures in the west. Rainfall is roughly the same all year, but is greatest in the west. This is because mountains and moist westerly winds combine to bring most rain to western areas.

Learning outcomes

By the end of this spread pupils should be able to:

- describe and explain the difference between weather and climate
- identify the factors affecting Britain's climate
- use maps to identify climate patterns across Britain.

Key vocabulary

- weather
- climate
- North Atlantic Drift

Learning objectives

On this spread pupils should learn:

- why temperature varies across Britain
- that rainfall varies considerably across Britain.

Skills builder

One of the outcomes of this spread is that pupils should be to identify patterns on maps. Using the maps of temperature and rainfall will enable them to do this. Work with pupils to help them to see the patterns.

- The map of summer temperatures shows a clear gradation in temperature from cooler in the north to warmer in the south.
- In winter, temperatures are colder in the east and milder in the west.
- The map of average annual rainfall shows that the west of Britain is far wetter than the east.
- The cooling effect of the Irish Sea can be seen in summer.
- The warming effect of the Irish Sea can be seen in winter.

Further discussion suggestions

- Why do many people retire to the south-west of England?
- Which part of the United Kingdom would you go to if you wanted to go skiing?
- Which part of the United Kingdom has the biggest difference in temperature between summer and winter?

Answers to activities

1. Weather is the day-to-day condition of the atmosphere. Climate is the average of weather conditions (measured over a period of 30 years).

2. a Summers in Britain are **warmer** than winter. The warmest weather is in the **south** and temperatures get lower (decrease) towards the **north**.

   b Winters in Britain are colder than summer. The warmest weather is in the west and temperatures get lower (decrease) towards the east.

3. Reasons for temperature differences include: wind direction, ocean currents, latitude, height, distance from the sea.

4. a Three wettest towns (wettest first): Fort William (2,000 mm), Glasgow (1,560 mm), Keswick (1,480 mm).

   Three driest towns (driest first): London (510 mm), Newcastle (630 mm), Norwich (650 mm).

   b The map shows that places in the west of Britain are much wetter than the east. The wettest place on the map is Fort William in north-west Scotland. It has 2,000 mm of rainfall a year.

   The driest places are in the east. London is the driest place shown on the map with 510 mm of rainfall a year.

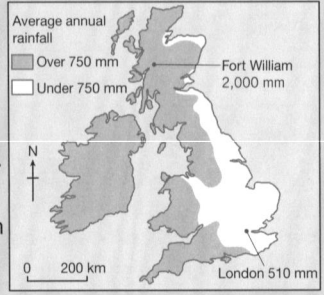

5. b Pupils' maps should match descriptions and locations on their map as follows.

   - (B) Mild summers, cold winters, dry.
   - (C) Warm summers, mild winters, quite wet.
   - (D) Warm summers, cold winters, dry.

   c Area (A) has mild summers, mild winters and is wet all year because:
   - it is at a high latitude (in summer the sun warms the south more than the north)
   - this is an area of predominantly high land, and temperatures decrease with height (e.g. summers are cooler than if land were low-lying)
   - the North Atlantic Drift helps to stop temperatures falling in the winter
   - the prevailing wind is from the south-west and brings rain all year.

   d and e

   Responses will depend on which area of the country you are located in. Pupils should use the reasons in diagram C to explain the climate.

2 Weather and climate

Pupil Book pages 24–25

How does it rain?

About this spread

On this spread pupils will find out that the answer to the question 'How does it rain?' is very simple. Moist air rises, cools, condenses and forms clouds, which leads to precipitation. Air is caused to rise by going over mountains (giving relief rainfall), by being warmed (convectional rainfall) or warm air might rise over cold air (frontal rainfall).

Learning objectives

On this spread pupils should learn:
- how rain forms
- about the three main types of rainfall – relief, convectional and frontal rain.

Learning outcomes

By the end of this spread pupils should be able to:
- use a labelled diagram to describe how rain forms
- explain the formation of relief, convectional and frontal rain
- explain why some places are wetter than others

Key vocabulary

- condensation
- relief rainfall
- convectional rainfall
- frontal rainfall

Skills builder

In geography, pupils need to be able to describe and explain a range of different processes. On this spread they learn about the processes that lead to rainfall – how air rises, cools and condenses to form clouds, leading to rainfall. They can use Activity 2 to check their understanding.

When they reach GCSE-level pupils will learn the same process but in more detail, e.g. that condensation occurs when air has cooled to dew point, and that as air descends and warms it is able to pick up more moisture and begin the rain-making process again. This could be introduced to higher-ability pupils where appropriate.

Further discussion suggestions

- Why does steam from a boiled kettle cause condensation on a nearby window?
- Why is the area east of the Pennines drier than the west?
- Why is south-east England more likely to suffer drought than south-west England in summer?

Answers to activities

1. Clouds are made up of tiny drops of moisture called cloud droplets.

   Precipitation is rain, snow and other forms of moisture in the sky.

   Condensation happens when water vapour changes to water.

2. Pupils' diagrams should be similar to diagram A on page 24 of the pupil book.

3. a–e

4. Seathwaite is in the west of England, in the mountainous Lake District, and receives relief rainfall. Newcastle is on the east side of England. Moist air brought by the prevailing winds is forced to rise over the mountains in the Lake District. As it rises, it cools, condenses and forms clouds. It then rains in the Lake District – including over Seathwaite. Once the air has passed over the mountains of the Lake District it descends and warms. By the time the air reaches Newcastle rain has stopped falling.

Relief rainfall

Precipitation occurs, usually in the form of rain
Condensation occurs and clouds form
Air rises and cools
Warm, moist air
Mountain

Air is forced to rise over mountains.

Convectional rainfall

Precipitation occurs – showery rain and thunderstorms
Condensation occurs and clouds form
Warm air rises and cools
Sun's heat
Ground is warmed by the sun

The ground surface is heated by the sun. The air above it warms up and rises.

Frontal rainfall

Precipitation occurs, usually in the form of rain
Condensation occurs and clouds form
Rising air cools
Warm
Cold
Warmer, lighter air rises over colder, heavier air

When a mass of warm air meets cooler air, it rises up and over the colder, heavier air.

2 Weather and climate

Pupil Book pages 26–27

Forecasting the weather – anticyclones

About this spread

The aim of this spread is to give pupils a better understanding of weather forecasts, focusing on anticyclones. Satellite images are used in weather forecasting, and the satellite image on this spread shows an anticyclone. The emphasis is on the weather associated with an anticyclone rather than on how they form. It is sufficient for pupils to know that in anticyclones cool air descends and air pressure is increased.

Learning outcomes

By the end of this spread pupils should be able to:
- forecast the weather using a basic weather map
- describe the features of an anticyclone
- understand the weather associated with an anticyclone.

Key vocabulary

- weather forecast
- anticyclone
- pressure

Learning objectives

On this spread pupils should learn:
- how anticyclones form (in brief)
- about the weather associated with anticyclones.

Skills builder

When writing their weather forecasts in Activity 6, pupils will be practising their written English. Although the weather forecast is going to be read out, pupils' spelling should be accurate and they should use correct punctuation and grammar. The correct geographical terms should be used appropriately. These should include the use of compass points to identify the different parts of the British Isles. The discussion should show an ability to take an overview of the whole country, as well as recognizing variations between the different parts of the country.

Further discussion suggestions

- Why do the spacing of the isobars on Figure D suggest that the winds will be very light?
- Why does the general absence of clouds have a big effect on the temperature when the British Isles is experiencing anticyclonic conditions?
- How may traffic conditions be affected by an anticyclone in winter?

Answers to activities

1 Pupils' responses will vary depending on where in the country they are. They should mention temperature, cloud cover/sunshine, wind speed and direction in their forecasts.

2 a Individual pupil's responses will vary, but it may be useful for them to know what the next day's weather will be like if they are taking part in a sports event, going on holiday, having a day out, going on a school trip, etc.

  b Pupil's lists may vary, but the people mentioned on this spread are:
  - **Farmers** The weather may affect planting crops, harvesting or other outdoor jobs done on a farm.
  - **Fishermen** It may be dangerous for them to go out to sea if it is likely there will be a storm or gales.
  - **Aircraft pilots** They may need to know if fog, ice or snow is likely, which make take-off and landing difficult.
  - **Builders** If they are working outdoors, they will want to know if high winds or rain are likely, which could make their work hazardous.

3 Satellites can allow forecasters to see weather systems from a great distance. They allow forecasters to track weather systems to predict how they will affect our weather.

4 **a** and **b**

Pupils should sketch the anticyclone in diagram D and complete the following paragraph:

Anticyclones are areas of **high** pressure which form when **cool** air sinks. They usually cover **large** areas and give **long** periods of fine settled weather.

5

	Summer	Winter
Temperatures	High	Low
Cloud cover	Few clouds, mainly clear skies	Clear skies
Wind speed	Light winds	Light winds
Wind direction	Winds blow clockwise	Winds blow clockwise
Rain	No rain	No rain
Other features	Fine settled sunny weather (with 'heat wave conditions')	Frost and fog

6 Pupils' weather forecasts should mention an anticyclone (a high-pressure weather system) and the type of weather this brings: fine settled mainly sunny weather, few clouds, with temperatures up to 26 °C, light winds, etc. Forecasts should be a maximum of 150 words.

2 Weather and climate

Pupil Book pages 28–29

Forecasting the weather – depressions

About this spread

The aim of this spread is to give pupils a better understanding of weather forecasts, focusing on depressions. Satellite images are used in weather forecasting, and the satellite image on this spread shows a depression. The emphasis is on the weather associated with a depression rather than on how depressions form. It is sufficient for pupils to know that in depressions warm air rises and air pressure is reduced.

Learning objectives

On this spread pupils should learn:

- how depressions develop
- that depressions usually move across Britain from west to east
- the sequence of weather associated with a depression.

Learning outcomes

By the end of this spread pupils should be able to:

- recognise a depression on a satellite image
- understand that depressions are the most common weather system affecting Britain
- describe the weather associated with a depression and explain why it changes.

Key vocabulary

- depression
- front
- isobar

Skills builder

The Skills builder on page 12 refers to the use of photos as a core geographical skill and should include satellite photos. Satellite photos are often used to show pupils weather systems, including depressions and anticyclones, and they need to be able to interpret what the photos show. It is useful if the pupils are given the opportunity to work with a map and a photo or satellite image of the same area. They should appreciate, however, the difference in scale of the map and the photo or satellite image.

Pupils are likely to come across satellite images in other areas, e.g. when looking at land use, or when looking at areas of vegetation cover and vegetation loss (deforestation). See pages 116–117 of the pupil book for more information on using satellite images in general. Pupils should be made aware that some satellite images are given false colours to represent different uses of the land. The colours often bear no relationship to the colour of the feature on the ground so pupils must therefore make full use of the key provided.

Further discussion suggestions

- How well does the weather forecast on the TV accurately predict the actual weather that occurs in the school's area when a depression passes over?
- Contact the Met Office to fax the school an actual satellite image at the time of the lesson and use it to relate directly to the weather conditions outside the classroom.

2 Weather and climate

Pupil Book pages 28–29

Forecasting the weather – depressions *(continued)*

Answers to activities

1 Depressions are areas of **low** pressure which form when air **rises**. They usually move across Britain from **west** to **east** and bring most of our **cloud** and **rain**.

2 Depressions are areas of low pressure. As the diagram shows, when air pressure is low the air is usually rising.

As it rises, it cools and condenses, forming clouds and giving rain (see diagram opposite).

3 Pupils' answers should include a sketch of diagram B on page 28 of the pupil book, along with the table below.

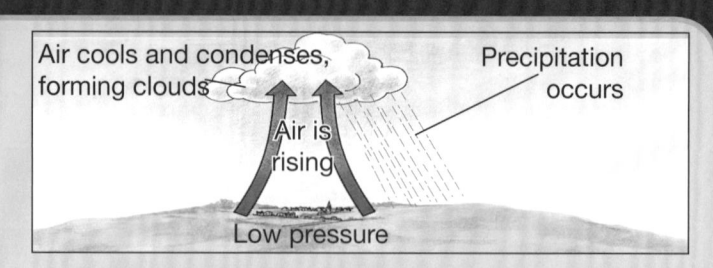

General features	Weather
Low pressure	Unsettled weather
Rising air, clouds form	Strong winds
Winds blow anti-clockwise	Fronts bring belts of cloud and rain
Usually travels from west to east	Storms
Brings a sequence of weather	

4 a **6 a.m.** Cloudy with rain. Strong southerly winds.

12 midday Cloudy with rain. Warmer. Winds have changed direction and now blow from the south-west.

6 p.m. Dry and mainly fine. Colder, less windy, with winds from the north-west.

b The weather at X has changed throughout the day as the depression passes over. At 6 a.m. the warm front is about to pass over X. By 12 midday the warm front has passed over, and X is in an area of warm air. The cold front is on its way. By 6 p.m. the cold front has passed as the depression heads east.

c and d

Pupils' responses will depend on where you are located. Their descriptions of the weather should be similar in format to those written for Bristol on diagram D.

5 a, b and c

Pupils are asked to trace the outline of Britain and mark and label the features shown on the photo here.

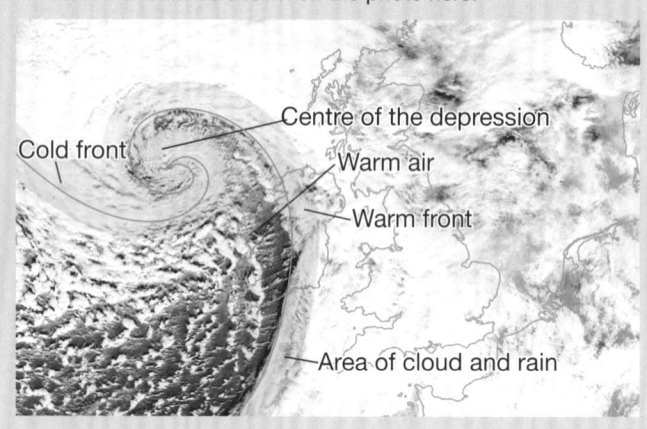

d The weather across the whole of Britain is cloudy. It is likely to be raining. Wind will be strong and probably blowing from the south or south-east.

2 Weather and climate

Pupil Book pages 30–33

The weather enquiry

About this spread

The weather enquiry is intended to be used at the end of the Weather and climate unit, and provides an opportunity to assess pupils' progress. Also see the self-assessment worksheet in Appendix 1 on page 61.

Learning outcomes

By the end of these spreads pupils should be able to:
- interpret climate graphs
- use a range of maps
- describe weather and climate in different regions
- make decisions using information in a variety of forms.

How can enquiries help with assessment?

For each enquiry in *Foundations* there is a checklist in the appendices. The checklist provides pupils with success criteria so that they know what is expected in order to produce high-quality answers and improve in the future. The checklist can be used in two ways:

- Pupils can use these as they go along, to check that they are meeting the success criteria for the enquiry.
- They can be used for assessment either by you, as the teacher, or another pupil, for peer marking. Any element that is not ticked provides evidence that the pupil has not met all of the criteria.

Learning objectives

On these spreads pupils should learn:
- what an enquiry is
- how to collect and present information on Britain's weather and climate
- how to write a conclusion to the enquiry.

What is the weather enquiry about?

This enquiry draws together pupils' work on weather and climate, and asks them to investigate what the differences are in weather and climate across Britain. Their task is to reply to a letter that asks them to provide weather and climate information for Oban, Aviemore, Plymouth and Cambridge, and to decide which place would suit the needs of different families.

Their enquiry should include:
- an introduction to explain what it is about
- a description of Britain's weather and climate (which could include a map)
- a conclusion in the form of a letter, which would explain their findings and include their decisions on which place is best suited to each family.

Differentiation suggestions

For lower-ability pupils
- Work with pupils to make sure they are clear about what they need to do, and the stages they need to go through in the enquiry.
- Provide pupils with a copy of the table in Part 2 of the enquiry, which is partially completed (see page 32 of the pupil book).
- Provide pupils with a completed table for one of the families in Part 3.
- You could provide a blank map and a writing frame for the letter to use for the conclusion to the enquiry.

For higher-ability pupils
- Pupils could use the internet to find out more detailed information on Britain's weather and climate. They could use the BBC weather website (www.bbc.co.uk/weather) and the Met Office (www.metoffice.gov.uk).
- Ask pupils to justify why the other locations were not suitable for each family.

2 Weather and climate

Pupil Book pages 30–40

The weather enquiry (continued)

Table for use in Part 2

Britain's weather	Oban (north and west)	Aviemore (north and east)	Plymouth (south and west)	Cambridge (south and east)
January temp. (°C)	4 °C			
July temp. (°C)	14 °C			
January rainfall (mm)	145 mm			
July rainfall (mm)	125 mm			
Total rainfall (mm per year)	1,435 mm			
Rainy days (number per year)	Over 225			
July sunshine (hours per day)	Below 5 hours a day			
Snow lying (days per year)	10–30			
Average wind strength (description and km/h)	Windy 20–24 km/h			

Table for use in Part 3

The Jackson family	Oban (north and west)	Aviemore (north and east)	Plymouth (south and west)	Cambridge (south and east)
Cold winters (Jan. temp. below 3 °C)	✗	✓	✗	✗
Warm summers (July temp. 15–20 °C)	✗	✗	✓	✓
Dry (less than 175 rainy days)	✗	✗	✗	✓
Quite sunny in summer (6–7 hrs per day)	✗	✗	✓	✓
Very little wind (below 16 km/h)	✗	✗	✗	✓
TOTAL	0	1	2	4

3 River flooding

What causes a river to flood?

Pupil Book pages 36–37

About this spread

This spread introduces pupils to the idea of river flooding, which is the focus of the rest of this unit. Rivers flood if water cannot soak into the ground. Pupils will find out that there are a number of physical and human factors that can increase the risk of rivers flooding.

Learning outcomes

By the end of this spread pupils should be able to:
- explain why rivers flood
- describe the physical and human factors that increase the risk of flooding.

Key vocabulary

- river flood
- impermeable
- deforestation
- urbanisation

Learning objectives

On this spread pupils should learn:
- river flooding is most likely after heavy rain or rapid snowmelt
- the risk of flooding increases when water is unable to soak into the ground
- human activities can increase the risk of flooding.

Skills builder

Pupils need to develop a wide range of geographical skills and these include the ability to draw and label diagrams. Their diagrams do not need to be works of art, but they do need to be clear and straightforward. Activity 1 on page 37 of the pupil book provides a diagram for pupils to copy. They need to work out where to put the labels they are given.

In Activity 3 pupils could copy the diagrams and add annotations to explain how cutting down trees and building towns can make flooding worse. You will need to tell pupils that annotations are labels that explain things, they are not just descriptive.

Further discussion suggestions

- Do you think that humans have increased the dangers of flooding?
- Are physical or human factors more important in causing rivers to flood?
- Are flood risks greater in a town or in the countryside?

Answers to activities

1 a and b

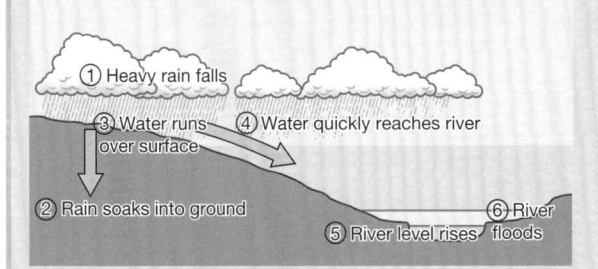

① Heavy rain falls
② Rain soaks into ground
③ Water runs over surface
④ Water quickly reaches river
⑤ River level rises
⑥ River floods

(1) Heavy rain falls
(2) Rain soaks into ground
(3) Water runs over surface
(4) Water quickly reaches river
(5) River level rises
(6) River floods

2 Four factors that increase the risk of flooding are as follows:

Rock and soil type Impermeable rocks and soil do not allow water to soak through them. Any rain that falls will remain near the surface.

Very wet/saturated soil If rain has been falling for a length of time, the soil may become saturated. Any further rain is unable to soak into the ground and remains on the surface.

Very dry soil Soil can become very hard in dry weather and will build up a crust. Rain is unable to soak through the crust and remains on the surface.

Steep slopes Rain falling on steep slopes runs quickly downhill towards a river. Most of it stays on the surface as it has little time to soak into the ground.

3 a and b

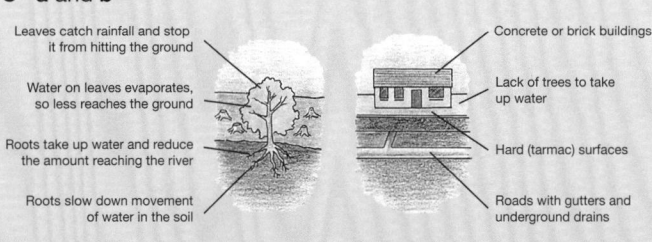

Leaves catch rainfall and stop it from hitting the ground
Water on leaves evaporates, so less reaches the ground
Roots take up water and reduce the amount reaching the river
Roots slow down movement of water in the soil

If trees are cut down, more rain reaches the ground and finds its way into the river more quickly, making flooding worse.

Concrete or brick buildings
Lack of trees to take up water
Hard (tarmac) surfaces
Roads with gutters and underground drains

Rain falling onto hard surfaces can't soak into the ground. Gutters and drains carry the water quickly into the river, increasing the risk of flooding.

4 Please see page 55 for answers to activities on page 109 of the pupil book.

3 River flooding

Pupil Book pages 38–39

Floods in the UK, 2012

About this spread

The flooding that hit York in 2012 is used as a case study on this spread. This follows on naturally from the spread on causes of river flooding on pages 36 and 37. It allows the pupils to relate the general causes and effects of river flooding to a real-world example. The pupils will be shown that the flooding in York was the result of both physical and human geographical factors, many of which took place well away from the actual city of York.

Learning objectives

On this spread pupils should learn:

- how to extract information from a written text with illustrations
- there were many factors responsible for the flooding in York
- there were many effects of the flooding.

Learning outcomes

By the end of the spread pupils should be able to:

- explain that physical and human factors, often far away from the city, were responsible for the flooding in York
- describe the long-term and short-term effects of the flooding in York
- relate generic factors causing flooding to a real-world example.

Skills builder

The case study gives the opportunity for pupils to extract information from a written source. This can be done by colour coding the text in order to classify the information into causes and effects. Lower-ability pupils could be given a partly completed table with the headings provided and at least one example of each already filled in. The photographs should be used to develop pupils' skills in description by getting them to use terminology such as foreground and background when identifying features. The descriptions should be related to information extracted from the text.

Further discussion suggestions

- Are there any similarities in the flooding in York with a flooding event which has taken place more recently or locally to the school? (You could use the extreme weather video from Kerboodle to support this question.)
- Do you think that people should be allowed to build where they like?
- Is flooding becoming more common in the UK?

Answers to activities

1.
   a. September 2012
   b. River Ouse
   c. Rivers Nidd, Swale and Wharfe
   d. York, Barlby and Selby
   e. Pennines and the North York Moors

2. Natural causes:
   - A month's amount of rain fell in 24 hours.
   - Rivers burst their banks and flooded surrounding areas.
   - The ground became full of water and could take no more.

   Human causes:
   - Ploughing of fields allows water to drain quickly into rivers.
   - Housing estates built on flood plains put more homes at risk.
   - Cutting down trees on valley slopes causes more rain to reach rivers.

3. Pupils' responses may vary, but should be along the following lines.

   The river Ouse was at its highest level for 387 years and reached a record high of 6.2 metres above its usual level. Over a thousand properties were flooded and hundreds of people had to leave their homes. Many lost all their belongings and when the floods went down, the houses were left with everything covered in a thick layer of foul-smelling mud. There will be a big rise in insurance premiums and many people may not be able to get their homes insured again. Many roads were blocked and people could not get to work from the villages outside the city.

4. Pupils' responses may vary, but should be along the following lines.

   A. The river has burst its banks and covered the road and pavements running along the bank. The water has flooded the nearby pub, the King's Arms. The water appears to be about a metre deep as it has come to the top of the bollard along the pavement and halfway up a road sign. In the background, where the land is slightly higher, sandbags have been placed and cars have been parked to keep them out of the flood waters.

   B. A woman is filling sandbags that have been placed alongside the railings to try and prevent water from the river getting into the buildings. This does not seem to have been totally successful as large pumps are being used to put water back into the river. A hose pipe is being used to drain the houses, which also suggests that they have been flooded.

3 River flooding

Pupil Book pages 40–41

How does the UK cope with floods?

About this spread

Serious flooding seems to be happening more often in the UK. This spread tells pupils about the role of the Environment Agency in relation to flooding. It is their job to monitor rainfall, river levels and sea conditions and to issue warnings when flooding is likely.

Learning outcomes

By the end of this spread pupils should be able to:

- describe how the Environment Agency reduces the risk, and limits the effects, of flooding
- understand that rich countries like the UK can afford schemes to reduce the effects of flooding

Key vocabulary

- **Environment Agency**

Learning objectives

On this spread pupils should learn:

- about the role of the Environment Agency in predicting flooding
- about the warnings and advice provided by the Environment Agency.

Skills builder

Pupils need to be able to research information for themselves by using the internet, but they should have guidance in doing so. When asking them to research information, provide them with the websites they need to use. This will save time searching for the information and allow them to focus their search. Activity 4 in the pupil book asks pupils to search for information on the Environment Agency website.

Further discussion suggestions

- What would you include in your own personal flood plan?
- Should new houses in areas at risk from flooding be built on stilts?
- How can a reservoir and its dam be used to control a river's flow?

Answers to activities

1 a The Environment Agency can help to reduce the risk of flooding by identifying areas at risk from rivers or the sea, and those areas where flooding would cause most damage. This can be done by recommending building flood defences, monitoring rainfall, river levels and sea conditions to see if flooding is likely.

  b The Environment Agency can help to limit the worst effects of flooding by issuing warnings and home visits (for those in most danger) when floods are expected; alerting the emergency services to provide help for those most in need; providing advice on what to do before, during and after a flood.

2 The Severe Flood Warning would have been issued as there was danger to life and property (evidenced by the fact that the emergency services had to rescue people trapped in buildings and on rooftops; over a thousand homes and businesses were flooded and hundreds of people were forced to leave their homes).

3 Family Flood Plan: pupils' responses may vary, but should be along the following lines.

Know how to contact each other in case family members become separated/can't get home/their home is flooded.

Put together an emergency flood kit to keep the family warm, safe and fed during the flood.

Know how to turn off power supplies. It is dangerous to use electricity and gas when a house is flooded.

Put emergency numbers in a safe place so they are easy to find during an emergency.

Understand the flood warning system so they know how imminent, and how severe, flooding is likely to be. Listen to the local radio programme for current local information on the flood situation.

4 a and b

Pupils' responses will vary. They should use information on this page as well as information from the Environment Agency website.

3 River flooding

Pupil Book pages 42–43

How can the risk of flooding be reduced?

About this spread

Serious flooding seems to be happening more often in the UK. The aim of this spread is to introduce pupils to the variety of flood prevention schemes that can be used to reduce the flood risk (but without complicating it by using the terms 'hard' and 'soft' engineering). It also considers the idea that flooding should be allowed to happen, but in a controlled way. Pupils are asked to think about what different people's reactions would be if flooding was allowed to happen naturally.

Learning outcomes

By the end of this spread pupils should be able to:
- describe different methods used to reduce the risk of flooding
- explain why not everyone is in favour of allowing rivers to flood naturally.

Key vocabulary

- flood prevention schemes
- embankment

Learning objectives

On this spread pupils should learn:
- about different methods used to reduce the flood risk
- that different people may have differing views about flood prevention schemes.

Skills builder

In Activity 3 on page 43 of the pupil book, pupils need to decide whether people would be for or against allowing rivers to flood naturally. They also need to give reasons for their answer. Giving reasons, or justifying answers, will encourage pupils to think more deeply about their responses to questions, because they need to offer something in support of their answers. This is a skill that is useful not just in geography but across a wide range of subjects.

Further discussion suggestions

- How can flood prevention schemes destroy the natural environment?
- How can flood prevention schemes protect wildlife?
- Why was the Thames Barrier built?

Answers to activities

1. Pupils' star diagrams should look similar to the one below.

   Note that pupils are only asked to write one sentence to describe each method of reducing the flood risk.

   Reducing the risk of flooding

   - **Widening and deepening channels** The banks and bed of a river can be dredged to make the channel wider and deeper. This means it will hold more water, so flooding is less likely.
   - **Concrete linings** Lining river channels with concrete means water flows more quickly away from towns and cities.
   - **Straightening channels** Straightening the river will speed up the flow of water and take it to the sea or lake more quickly.
   - **Dams** A dam traps water and stores it in a reservoir. Water is released in a controlled way.
   - **Overflow channels** Water is allowed to flow into temporary storage areas or out to sea through overflow channels.
   - **Forests** Planting trees slows down the flow of water and reduces the amount reaching the river.
   - **Embankments** A river's banks can be built up with earth or concrete. This has the effect of making the river channel deeper to allow it to hold more water.
   - **Allow flooding** Let flooding happen – but in a controlled way. Allow excess water to collect in safe areas. Keep river bends (don't straighten them) to slow down the flow of water.

2. a Dams are likely to cost the most. They are massive structures that take a long time to build.

   b Allowing flooding to happen costs the least. Nothing needs to be built or altered, so minimal costs are involved.

   c Building dams. As the water level builds up in the reservoir behind the dam, farmland and houses are likely to be drowned.

   d Dams and the creation of reservoirs are likely to use up the most land.

   e Allowing flooding to happen protects the natural environment – allowing the river to maintain its natural course means only natural processes will occur and flooding will continue as it has in the past.

3. Local farmer is **against**

   Flooding could destroy crops.

   Flood protection manager is **for**

   Natural flooding can improve water quality and be a far cheaper option than many other flood preventions measures.

   Bird watcher is **for**

   Natural flooding can help to support wildlife.

3 River flooding

Pupil Book pages 44–45

The river flooding enquiry

About this spread

The river flooding enquiry is intended to be used at the end of the river flooding unit and provides an opportunity to assess pupils' progress. Also see the self-assessment checklist in Appendix 2 on page 62.

Learning objectives

On this spread pupils should learn:
- to evaluate different flood protection schemes.

Learning outcomes

By the end of this spread pupils should be able to:
- interpret and use a map to make decisions about a geographical issue
- decide on the most appropriate scheme to protect the Doveton valley from flooding
- assess how different people would react to the chosen scheme.

What is the river flooding enquiry about?

This enquiry enables pupils to use what they have learned about reducing the risk of flooding, and flood protection, in the context of a given location. Their task is to assess four different possible schemes to decide which is best for the Doveton valley. They then need to consider how different people would react to their chosen scheme.

Their enquiry should include:
- an introduction to explain what it is about
- a completed table that will allow them to decide which scheme to choose, with an explanation of what the table is about
- a conclusion that describes their chosen scheme, explains how it will protect the valley from flooding, and gives the views of four different people from the valley.

How can enquiries help with assessment?

For each enquiry in *Foundations* there is a checklist in the appendices. The checklist provides pupils with success criteria so that they know what is expected in order to produce high-quality answers and improve in the future.

- Pupils can use these as they go along, to check that they are meeting the success criteria for the enquiry.
- They can be used for assessment either by you, as the teacher, or another pupil, for peer marking. Any element that is not ticked provides evidence that the pupil has not met all of the criteria.

Differentiation suggestions

For lower-ability pupils
- Work with pupils to make sure they are clear about the steps they need to go through to complete the enquiry.
- Recap the work done on pages 42 and 43 of the pupil book on how the risk of flooding can be reduced and the different strategies that can be used. Make sure pupils are clear that different schemes can be used together.
- Provide pupils with a copy of Table A, which is partially completed (see below).
- You could give pupils an example of why one of the local residents, e.g. Trudy Trout, would not be in favour of Scheme A. In her case, the dam would create a reservoir that would flood large amounts of land, probably including that on which the caravan park sits. She would lose her livelihood as a result of this scheme.

For higher-ability pupils
- Ask these pupils to explain why they rejected the other schemes.
- They could also suggest additions to their chosen scheme (e.g. planting trees in the drainage basin above Crofton).
- They could be given the table with two or three of the 'Factors to consider' omitted so they could come up with their own suggestions.
- They could consider another person or group of people who may be affected and suggest which scheme they could favour.
- They could organise a role play with different interested parties arguing for a particular scheme. Lower-ability pupils could then vote to decide which scheme should be implemented.

Table A

Factors to consider	Scheme A	Scheme B	Scheme C	Scheme D
Prevents all flooding	✓	✗	✗	✗
Stops flooding in Crofton	✓	✗	✓	✓
No homes lost	✗	✓	✓	✓
No roads submerged				
No grazing land lost				
No good farmland lost				
Helps with irrigation				
Helps protect wildlife				
Not too expensive				
Total				

4 Urbanisation

Pupil Book pages 48–49: How were the sites for early settlement chosen?

About this spread

On this spread pupils will learn that the sites for early settlements were chosen for their advantages. In the activities, pupils are asked to decide which site they would choose for a settlement in Ancient Britain when all the sites have advantages and disadvantages. Pupils will also learn, by looking at Warkworth in Northumberland, that, over a period of time, the original advantages of a site become less important.

Learning outcomes

By the end of this spread pupils should be able to:
- define the term 'site'
- explain how sites for early settlements were chosen
- explain why the advantages of particular sites change over time.

Key vocabulary

- site

Learning objectives

On this spread pupils should learn:
- that sites were chosen for their advantages
- that a site's advantages can change over time.

Skills builder

Using and interpreting photos is a key geographical skill, and the photo of Warkworth on page 49 of the pupil book provides an excellent example of how a photo can be interpreted. You could provide pupils with a photo of your own settlement and work with them to interpret the photo in terms of the settlement's site, using the advantages for sites listed in diagram A. Pupils could then annotate their photo with the reasons why your settlement developed on its site. The photo could also be the basis of a sketch map which could be annotated in a similar way by identifying the site's advantages. If pupils are familiar with Ordnance Survey maps then they could be used in conjunction with the photograph, initially at a scale 1 : 50,000 and then perhaps at 1 : 25,000, which would show more detail.

Further discussion suggestions

- Using Warkworth as an example, explain why the river was important for the defence of the town.
- Explain the choice of site for Warkworth Castle.
- What are the disadvantages of the site of Warkworth today?

Answers to activities

Page 48

1. 'Site' is the actual land on which the settlement is built,

2. a Natural advantages include: **A** protection (good views from hilltop), flat land (e.g. for building on); **B** shelter (from wind and rain), building materials (some bare rock); **C** building materials (wood), supply of wood (for fuel); **D** not too far from water (but not too much water), gentle slope/good soil (good for growing crops), close to woodland (for building materials and fuel); **E** flat land, close to river (for accessibility and water supply).

   b Natural disadvantages include: **A** no water, no shelter (from wind and rain); **B** steep slope (no flat land for building, growing crops, etc.), far from water; **C** no view (so no warning of attack), not close to water; **D** not much view (so more danger of attack); **E** Flat marshy land (too much water – liable to flood/not good for crop growing), far from source of good building materials.

   c Pupils might choose different sites but must give three reasons for their choice, which should include the site's natural advantages.

3. Some suitable websites or other resources could be given to the pupils as a starting point.

Page 49

1.

Defence
Castle built on steep rocky outcrop for defence
River provided good defence on three sides

Food and water
Good farming land nearby
River provided good water supply

→ Site advantages of Warkworth ←

Building materials
Nearby rock outcrops provided building materials
Wood available for building

Building land
Firm, flat land, easy to build on
Dry site well above river flood level

2.

Original advantage	Why no longer important
River used for transport	Roads are far more commonly used for transport now
Good farming land nearby	Although we may consume some locally produced food, much of our food comes from elsewhere in the UK or from other parts of the world
Wood available for fuel and building	Wood is no longer a main source of fuel
Castle built on steep rocky outcrop for defence	We no longer need to protect ourselves from attack in this way
River provided good defence on three sides	We no longer need to protect ourselves from attack in this way
Nearby rocky outcrops provided good building materials	Although some local rock may still be used for building, most building materials are likely to come from elsewhere

4 Urbanisation

Pupil Book pages 50–51

What different settlement patterns are there?

About this spread

This spread defines the three main types of settlement patterns – dispersed, nucleated and linear – and illustrates them with three oblique aerial photos. The activities help pupils to recognise settlement patterns in an area of Devon on an Ordnance Survey (OS) map.

Learning objectives

On this spread pupils should learn:
- that there are three main types of settlement patterns
- how to use OS maps to recognise settlement patterns.

Learning outcomes

By the end of this spread pupils should be able to:
- understand the difference between dispersed, nucleated and linear settlements
- understand that the shape of a settlement is usually determined by the physical features of the surrounding area
- identify different settlement patterns on an OS map.

Key vocabulary

- settlement pattern
- dispersed settlement
- nucleated settlement
- linear settlement
- ribbon development

Skills builder

When studying geography, pupils need to be able to use and interpret maps at a variety of scales. The map included on page 51 of the pupil book is an OS map at 1:50,000. It has a partial key with it (note that a full key is included on the inside back cover of the pupil book).

The activities on page 51 will help pupils to develop their map work skills, both in terms of using grid references (use page 96 of the pupil book if pupils need reminding how to give four-figure grid references), and in identifying settlement patterns on a map.

Answers to activities

1 Pupils need to copy the settlement pattern drawings.

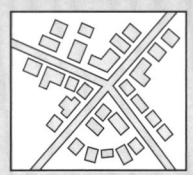

Nucleated buildings are closely grouped or clustered together. Nucleated settlements often grew up around a road junction (as here) or river crossing. Houses were built close together for safety.

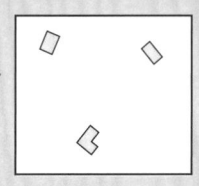

Dispersed buildings are well spread out. Dispersed settlements are often found in highland areas where people needed more land to grow crops or graze animals. It was not easy to build houses close together.

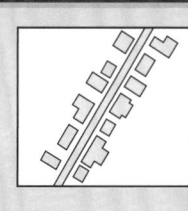

Linear settlements have a long narrow shape. They usually occur in a narrow valley, where there is little space to spread out, or along a road or either side of a river.

2 a and b

Village name	Map reference	Simple drawing	Settlement pattern
Bowden	7644		Dispersed
Slapton	8144		Nucleated
South Pool	7740		Linear
Cotmore	8041		Dispersed
Beeson	8140		Nucleated
Torcross	8242		Linear
Sherford	7744		Linear

c There are several other examples of nucleated and linear settlements pupils could choose. Ensure grid references are correct.

4 Urbanisation

Pupil Book pages 52–53

How do settlements change with time?

About this spread

This spread uses, as an example of how settlements change over a period of time, a village that has become suburbanised. Drawings show how the village might have been in the 1890s and how it had changed by the 2000s. Changes affect both the land use and the lives of various groups of people living there. Pupils are asked to consider the consequences of a further change in the village.

Learning objectives

On this spread pupils should learn:

- the ways that settlements change over time
- that different groups of people are affected in different ways by changes in settlements.

Skills builder

For geography, pupils need to be able to use different sources of information and identify changes. On this spread, pupils are asked to identify changes by analysing diagrams of a village, and to decide whether different groups of people will be in favour or against further changes.

Learning outcomes

By the end of this spread pupils should be able to:

- define the terms 'shape', 'function' and 'land use' related to settlements
- describe the changes in a rural landscape over the last century
- explain why people will have differing opinions about changes in settlements.

Further discussion suggestions

- What is a dormitory village?
- Are second houses in the countryside a problem?
- Why are many village shops and pubs being forced to close?

Key vocabulary

- function
- land use
- suburbanised

Answers to activities

1 a The shape of a settlement is related to the settlement pattern. Settlements can be dispersed (spread out), nucleated (buildings grouped together) or linear (long and narrow).

  b The function of a settlement is its purpose, e.g. market town, commuter village, etc.

  c The land use is simply what the land is used for, e.g. housing, industry, shops and offices.

2 The differences between the village in the 1890s and the 2000s include the following:

- The pond has been drained, with a by-pass built over it and around the village.
- A ribbon development of 1930s houses has been built adjacent to the by-pass.
- Other housing has been built on farmland (e.g. large brick houses opposite what was the village shop).
- The school and playground have been converted into a craft museum and car park.
- Housing has been converted into a restaurant (with adjacent car park).
- Farm workers' cottages have been converted into holiday homes.
- There is a new caravan park on the edge of the village.
- Farm buildings have been converted into homes.
- There is a new old people's home behind what was the village shop.
- The village shop has been converted into tea rooms.
- Lanes into the village have been widened into bigger roads.

4 Urbanisation

Pupil Book pages 52–53

How do settlements change with time? *(continued)*

Answers to activities

3 **Farmer** I made money by selling my land so that houses can be built. Now people walk on the land I still own.

Shopkeeper I might have to close as most people have cars to shop in town.

Bird watcher The extra noise frightens away the wildlife.

Teenager I have to travel 10 km to school. At night there is nothing to do.

Young married couple We are just married and cannot afford an expensive house.

Restaurant owner To get customers I have to provide food for townspeople. Villagers only want a drink.

Elderly person I came here for peace and quiet. Now I cannot drive into town and there are no buses.

Builder With all the new houses I have plenty of work to do.

4 a Some existing houses have changed from farm workers' cottages to holiday homes as the number of people working on the farms has declined and the farmers have diversified into providing holiday accommodation to supplement incomes. Redundant farm buildings are converted into homes. The overall number of homes has increased as people move out of towns and into villages – this has meant a change in the type of housing, e.g. 1930s housing and newer large brick houses.

b The school has closed and changed into a craft museum, probably because of declining numbers of children in the village as fewer people live and work there. People tend to shop at larger shops and supermarkets that open on the outskirts of towns. Therefore, there is not enough local trade to support a village shop, which is now a tea room. Old housing has been converted into a restaurant to cater for people coming from nearby towns.

c Some of the land around the village has been converted into a caravan park to cater for holidays (diversification from farming). Other land has been used for housing and to create a by-pass.

d Lanes have been widened into bigger roads to cater for the increase in motorised traffic. In the 1890s, there would only have been horse-drawn vehicles.

5 a **Builder**
Building more houses will provide him with work.

Farmer
Can make money selling land for building new houses.

Restaurant owner
People moving into new houses will provide more customers for the restaurant.

Shopkeeper
More people in the village means more customers in the shop.

b **Bird watcher**
More development will mean destruction of woodland and a decrease in habitats for birds, and an increase in noise level will scare birds away.

Young married couple
They would want smaller cheaper houses to be built, which they could afford.

Elderly person
More housing means more people and cars and less peace and quiet.

4 Urbanisation

Pupil Book pages 54–55

What are the benefits and problems of cash settlement growth?

About this spread

This spread uses two urban field sketches to help prompt pupils into identifying the benefits and problems resulting from urban growth. Many people all over the world still move to cities hoping for a better life, only to be disillusioned later.

Learning objectives

On this spread pupils should learn:
- that there are advantages and disadvantages associated with the growth of settlements.

Learning outcomes

By the end of this spread pupils should be able to:
- understand that people move to large cities because of the benefits they offer
- list the advantages and disadvantages of settlement growth
- describe some of the problems facing their own town or city and suggest some possible solutions.

Skills builder

This spread looks at some of the specific benefits and problems of the growth of settlements. We all live in settlements of one kind or another, and the benefits and problems identified on this spread might be found in our own town or city. Use Kerboodle or one of Activities 3 and 4 on page 55 to encourage pupils to apply what they are learning about to their own settlement. This will help them to see that geography is not just theory, but it is about real places with real issues that affect all of us.

Key vocabulary

- quality of life
- pollution
- urban

Further discussion suggestions

- What is urban decay?
- Why do some towns and cities need regenerating?
- Why do people build shantytowns on the outskirts of major cities in countries such as Brazil, Mexico and India?

Answers to activities

1. **a** Pupils will vary in their choice of which things they think are best about living in cities, and which things they think are worst. Most pupils are likely to choose things that are listed on the diagrams, or a variation on those. Some pupils may list other things from their own personal knowledge or experience.

   b Pupils' responses will depend on their own point of view.

2. Pupils' responses will vary, but they should give reasons for their answer, which may reflect the problems or benefits of settlements that they know.

3. **a, b** and **c**
   Responses will be totally dependent on your local situation.

4. Pupils may suggest a variety of ways in which problems may be tackled. Any suggestions are acceptable as long as they are (relatively) feasible.

4 Urbanisation

Pupil Book pages 56–57

Why are there different land use patterns in towns?

About this spread

This spread looks at land use patterns in a typical British town or city. Pupils are introduced to a simple urban land use model (it is the Burgess concentric ring model – but pupils do not need to know this) and consider the choice of housing for different people in different urban zones.

Learning objectives

On this spread pupils should learn:

- why there are different land use patterns in towns
- to interpret a simple model of urban land use.

Learning outcomes

By the end of this spread pupils should be able to:

- understand what an urban model shows
- understand that the main function, or land use, of an area may result from its age and the cost of the land
- name areas of their own local town for different land use zones.

Key vocabulary

- urban model
- **Central Business District (CBD)**
- inner city
- suburbs

Skills builder

Pupils will come across models in geography, as well as in other subjects. They need to understand that models are a simplified version of what happens in the real world. The urban model introduced here is the Burgess concentric ring model of urban land use. If pupils continue to study geography at GCSE level or beyond, they may well come across other urban models, both for rich and poor countries.

Show pupils a video clip on land use patterns in Oxford from the BBC Learning Zone (www.bbc.co.uk/learningzone/clips and search for clip 7784). The key thing pupils need to understand about models is that real life doesn't always fit the model that neatly – as the video clip of Oxford shows. However, in this case the model does give pupils something to base their understanding of urban land use patterns on.

Further discussion suggestions

- Why are the tallest buildings in a city found in the CBD?
- Why has there been a trend for people to move to the suburbs of a city? Who gets left behind?
- Why do factories in a city prefer to be located on industrial estates close to main roads or motorways?

Answers to activities

1 a and b

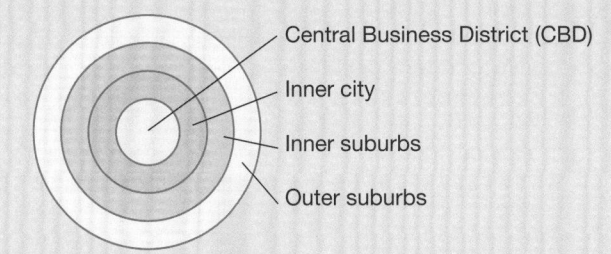

- Central Business District (CBD)
- Inner city
- Inner suburbs
- Outer suburbs

c Pupils should name an area of your local town or city for each of zones **A** (CBD), **B** (inner city), **C** (inner suburbs) and **D** (outer suburbs).

2 a First-time buyer = House 1.

Reasons include: price (it is the cheapest property); size (two bedrooms); location (close to CBD for jobs and entertainment); condition of property (young people more likely to want to take on modernisation).

b Family with two young children = House 3.

Reasons include: price (cheaper than a larger property in the outer suburbs); size (three bedrooms); location (close to primary school); cul-de-sac (will be quiet with little traffic and safer for children); garden (for children to play in).

c Children have left home and you have a good job = House 4.

Reasons include: price (it is the most expensive property, but those with a good job can afford it); type of house (large garden and conservatory for relaxation); location (close to golf course and local shopping centre, and in outer suburbs where it is quieter).

d **Time to retire** Pupils can choose any property as long as they give valid reasons for their choice.

e **Property for themselves as a teenager** Pupils can choose any property as long as they give valid reasons for their choice.

4 Urbanisation

Pupil Book pages 58–59

Why does land use in towns change?

About this spread

This spread uses London Docklands to show how land use changes with time. A photo of housing in the old docklands contrasts with the shining new office blocks. Pupils can describe the changes and analyse the reasons for them. They should also realise that while change may be good for some groups in the community, it can be bad for others, providing an opportunity for the development of values and attitudes.

Learning objectives

On this spread pupils should learn:

- that land use in towns and cities changes over time
- the reasons for changes in land use in towns and cities.

Learning outcomes

By the end of this spread pupils should be able to:

- explain why the functions and land use of London Docklands changed
- understand that changes in functions and land use affect different groups of people in different ways.

Skills builder

The work on this spread will help to build pupils' locational knowledge by focusing on the example of London Docklands. Show pupils a video clip of how London Docklands has changed. There's a good one on the BBC Learning Zone website (www.bbc.co.uk/learningzone/clips and search for clip 8317), which includes aerial shots and archive footage of the docks in action. Make sure pupils can locate London on a blank map of the UK, and that they can locate Docklands within London.

Using examples from your own local town or city will help pupils to understand that land use changes are not just theory but happen in places that they know about.

Further discussion suggestions

- How have the developments associated with the Olympic Games in 2012 affected this part of London?
- Using a local example of derelict land, suggest possible uses for the area.
- Set up a role-play scenario where the advantages and disadvantages of the different possible land uses are debated.

Answers to activities

1 a Docklands' early success was based on the fact that London was a busy port and Docklands had a thriving industrial zone.

 b Docklands declined because shipping in the Thames declined, so there weren't enough ships to support the port and its associated industries.

 c The docks were virtually abandoned and became derelict, and the number of jobs declined.

 d A typical house in the area was old, terraced and back-to-back. Many houses lacked bathrooms and indoor toilets. Many were in a bad state of repair.

 e 'A good community spirit' means that people know their neighbours and will help each other out. In Docklands, people were often in the same situation and would do things together.

2 Buildings
- Old docks and houses cleared
- Warehouses turned into flats
- Office blocks built

Industry/jobs
Old industry replaced with those using high technology, e.g. newspapers and financial firms

Transport
- Underground stations improved
- City Airport built
- Docklands Light Railway built

Environment
- Environment improved
- Trees planted
- Parklands created

3 a Winners include: **local shopkeepers** newcomers have more money to spend in their shops than local people; **financial managers** they have modern offices and can afford good-quality housing in the area, plus transport has been improved making it quick and easy to get into central London; **school leavers** they are being trained in IT so will be able to get jobs and stay in the area they grew up in.

 b Losers include: **young married couples** who cannot afford to buy a home in the area and so will have to move elsewhere; **elderly people** whose needs for hospitals and local services are not being met as money is being spent on houses and offices. Shopping is also expensive for them; **local people** can find that most of the jobs go to people from outside the area who are highly skilled, plus their community has been broken up as a result of the redevelopment.

4 Pupils should think about the impacts of the changes to London Docklands on different groups of people before they make their decision as to whether the changes have been good or bad. They must give reasons for their answer.

4 Urbanisation

Pupil Book pages 60–61

Where do we shop?

About this spread

This spread looks at where we shop for different types of goods. Pupils are introduced to the concept of convenience (low order) goods and comparison (high order) goods. In the activities, they decide where they would buy different types of goods. Page 61 includes a shopping survey activity. The aim of the survey is to compare shopping habits of people at the local shopping centre with those of people in the city centre.

Learning outcomes

By the end of this spread pupils should be able to:

- understand that there are different types of shops and shopping centres
- describe the differences between convenience and comparison goods
- understand that the larger the shopping centre, the greater the choice of shops and goods there are to buy.

Key vocabulary

- corner shop
- low order goods
- high order goods

Learning objectives

On this spread pupils should learn:

- that where we shop depends on what we need to buy and how often that product is needed.

Skills builder

Questionnaires and surveys can be used in a number of different topics in geography, and can also be used as a basic research tool. Asking questions helps pupils to learn about their surroundings and find out about other people's points of view.

The information collected is primary or first-hand data. Pupils should realise that, in a survey like this one, the more people interviewed the better the results will be. Make sure that pupils are aware of safety issues when conducting surveys.

See Chapter 6 of *Nelson Key Geography Interactions* for further information on questionnaires and surveys.

Further discussion suggestions

- How far away from home is your nearest convenience store?
- Can you name ten comparison goods in your home that were bought in a chain store?
- What is the influence of internet shopping on the high street?

Answers to activities

1 a Convenience goods are also called low order goods. They include things like food and newspapers, which people might buy every day and may buy in the nearest convenient place.

   b Comparison goods are also called high order goods. They include more expensive things like clothes and furniture, which we buy less often, and compare styles and prices before we buy.

   c A corner shop is a shop selling convenience goods such as food and newspapers.

2

Convenience goods	Comparison goods
Fish	Jumper
Milk	CD
Washing powder	Glasses
Fruit	Sports racquet
Bread	CD player
Chicken	Chair
Newspaper	Shoes
Sweets	TV
Basket of shopping	
Toilet roll	

3 Note that pupils' answers may vary because shopping centres and large supermarkets now sell many goods that used to be sold in shops in city centres – the following are suggested lists.

Corner shop: toilet roll; milk; bread; washing powder; fruit; newspaper; sweets.

Shopping centre: basket of shopping; fish; chicken.

City centre: jumper; CD; glasses; sports racquet; CD player; chair; shoes; TV.

4 Possible data presentation methods would be bar graphs and pie diagrams, which could either be hand drawn or produced using a spreadsheet on a computer. The most important aspect, however, would be the discussion of what the graphical representations show rather than the ability to draw them. The discussion of the findings should make use of the key geographical terms, such as 'convenience' and 'comparison'.

4 Urbanisation

Pupil Book pages 62–63

How has shopping changed?

About this spread

This spread looks at how shopping has changed both within the city centre and with the development of out-of-town shopping centres. It looks at the advantages and disadvantages of each. In the activities, pupils put themselves in the position of a shop owner whose business may be forced to close owing to the development of a new out-of-town shopping centre.

Learning outcomes

By the end of this spread pupils should be able to:

- understand that the city centre has always been the main shopping area in a town, but it is now often congested and expensive
- explain why modern out-of-town shopping centres are becoming increasingly popular.

Key vocabulary

- accessibility
- shopping malls

Learning objectives

On this spread pupils should learn:

- how the development of out-of-town shopping centres is threatening shops in the city centre.

Skills builder

In Activity 4, pupils need to write a letter or, better still, send an email. This provides them with an opportunity to produce a slightly longer piece of writing than most activities require, and so practise their written English. Their letter or email should include relevant information organised in a logical and coherent way. Their spelling, punctuation and grammar should be accurate so that it is clear what they are trying to say. Explain that the letter or email is to be sent to the local council, so it needs to be written in an appropriate style.

Further discussion suggestions

- What effect do supermarkets have on a town's local shops?
- Why have shopping malls become so popular, and where was the first one built in Britain?
- What advantages and disadvantages do inner city shopping centres have when compared with retail parks on the edge of town?

Answers to activities

1 **a and b**

   Pupils' answers will reflect your own local town or city. They should name the main street, shopping area or mall, and one department store, one nationwide supermarket and three specialist shops found there.

2 Pupils should copy sketch B (but this is not essential).

   a It has the largest number of shops, the biggest shops and most shoppers.

   b People are willing to travel long distances to the city centre because of the choice of goods they can buy there.

   c Different types of shops include department stores, nationwide supermarkets, chain stores and specialist shops.

   d Most of the main roads, bus routes and rail systems meet at the city centre, making it the easiest place for most people living in the town or city to reach.

   e Overcrowding and traffic congestion are the main problems.

   f Pedestrianised areas and covered shopping malls improve city centre shopping.

3 Pupils' posters should show the advantages of using a shopping centre. They can use the bullet points linked to photo C on page 63 of the pupil book.

4 Pupils' letters will vary, but they may include some of the following points.

   - The increased use of cars (by people visiting the shopping centre) will lead to increased air and noise pollution and traffic congestion.
   - Many local shops may be forced to close and people will lose their livelihoods.
   - Specialist independent shops may not survive.
   - Choice will be limited to what is available in the shopping centre and is likely to be dominated by national chains.

4 Urbanisation

Pupil Book pages 64–65

Traffic in urban areas – why is it a problem?

About this spread

This spread looks at the range of problems that traffic creates in urban areas – from traffic jams to pollution. The main cause of traffic problems is simply the number of cars on the roads. There are also other causes too, and pupils consider which they think are the worst.

Learning objectives

On this spread pupils should learn:

- about the problems traffic creates in urban areas
- about the causes of the traffic problems.

Learning outcomes

By the end of this spread pupils should be able to:

- list the problems caused by increased traffic in urban areas
- understand that the main causes of the problems are too many cars, rush-hour traffic and unsuitable roads
- describe the rate of change in the number of cars in the UK.

Key vocabulary

- congestion

Skills builder

In Activity 4, pupils are asked to compare a graph showing the increase in the number of cars in the UK from 1950 to 2010 using three model graphs. The models are simplified versions of what a graph based on real data might show. In this unit, pupils have already been introduced to an urban land use model on page 56 and, if they continue to study geography, they will come across other models, e.g. the demographic transition model, which shows how population changes over time. Pupils need to be clear that models are a useful tool, but that real life doesn't always fit the model that neatly.

Further discussion suggestions

- What is the school run and how does it add to traffic congestion?
- Why do many families now have two (or even three) cars?
- How can people be encouraged to drive smaller cars with lower exhaust emissions?

Answers to activities

1. Pupils' lists will vary, but they should choose from the problems given with photo A.

2. Pupils should write two letters to the MP.

    The businessman is more likely to be concerned about traffic jams, slow movement of people and goods resulting in a loss of business and money, and the lack of parking spaces.

    The local resident with two young children is likely to be concerned about noise and vibrations from traffic, the danger of accidents and harmful exhaust fumes.

3. Pupils' lists will vary, but they should choose from the information in drawing C.

4. a In 1950, there were approximately 3 million cars on Britain's roads. By 2010, there were just over 24 million.

    b The third (or last) graph in E looks most like that in graph D. There was a slow increase at first in the number of cars in the UK between 1950 and 2000. The number of cars increased rapidly later. (Higher-ability pupils may add that the rate of increase in car numbers slowed down between 1990 and 2010.)

4 Urbanisation

Pupil Book pages 66–67

Traffic in urban areas – is there a solution?

About this spread

Page 66 looks at the options for improving traffic in urban areas. These firstly consist of making improvements to cope with larger amounts of private transport, and secondly restricting private transport and improving public transport.

Page 67 looks at how public transport could be improved and uses the Manchester Metrolink as an example.

Learning objectives

On this spread pupils should learn:

- about some of the solutions to the problem of traffic in urban areas
- that the best way to tackle the problem may be by using different solutions together.

Learning outcomes

By the end of this spread pupils should be able to:

- understand that solving the problem of urban traffic is not easy
- describe how better public transport may be the best way to improve the movement of people without further damaging the environment
- describe a local traffic problem and suggest how it could be reduced.

Skills builder

The topic of traffic in urban areas is perfect for teaching in the context of your local town or city. Bringing in references to your local area helps to build pupils' understanding of how geography works in the real world. Use Kerboodle and Activity 6 on page 67, and your knowledge of local public transport to provide opportunities to learn about the local area. Get students to think about real-life solutions to help prevent traffic congestion.

Key vocabulary

- transport
- public transport

Further discussion suggestions

- What are the advantages and disadvantages of cars that run on electricity?
- Is a regular and widespread tram service and/or underground train network (as in Prague) a way to reduce traffic congestion in all cities?
- Can charging motorists to drive into city centres (as London does) be a way of reducing traffic congestion in all cities?

Answers to activities

1. **a** Public transport includes things like buses and trains, which don't belong to private individuals.
   b Private transport includes things like cars and motorbikes, which belong to private individuals.
   c Public transport: bus, train. Private transport: car, motorbike, bicycle.

2. Pupils' posters need to show the bad things about town centres, so could include: narrow streets; traffic jams; lack of parking; exhaust fumes, etc. Other types of transport that could be used include bicycles, buses, trains, trams, etc.

3.

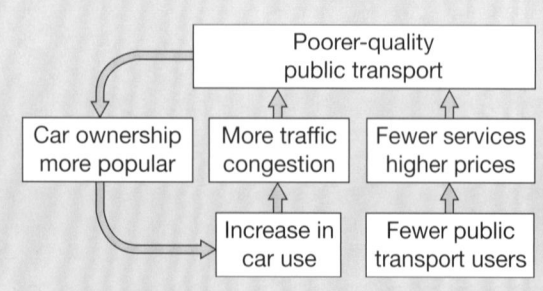

4. **a** Fares are subsidised; automatic ticket machines reduce costs; trams travel at speeds of up to 80 km/h.
   b Links with existing bus and rail routes.
   c It is powered by electricity (reducing noise and air pollution); takes up to 2.5 million car journeys a year off the road.

5. Disadvantages include: priority given to trams at traffic lights and road junctions, which may hold up other road users; trams run on tracks so routes are fixed, therefore not accessible to all.

6. Pupils may describe different traffic problems depending on where they live. Solutions suggested should be workable.

4 Urbanisation

Pupil Book pages 68–69

Where should the by-pass go?

About this spread

This spread consists of a decision-making exercise. Pupils are introduced to Haydon Bridge, a small town on the banks of the River Tyne between Newcastle and Carlisle. The amount of traffic passing through the town caused congestion, pollution and accidents. Pupils have to decide on the best route for the by-pass.

Learning outcomes

By the end of this spread pupils should be able to:

- work out the best route for the by-pass
- understand that cost, land availability and the environment have to be considered when choosing routes
- understand that no one route will satisfy everybody.

Key vocabulary

- by-pass

Learning objectives

On this spread pupils should learn:

- how to decide on the best route for a by-pass around a settlement.

Skills builder

In the activities on this spread pupils have to choose the best route for the by-pass. This is an example of a decision-making activity and pupils will come across these in other topics in geography. Pupils either need to be given a range of criteria (as in this case) to enable them to make a decision, or need to come up with the criteria themselves.

Other topics where pupils might meet decision-making activities could include:

- energy, e.g. deciding where wind farms should be built
- flooding, e.g. deciding what type of flood defences should be built
- coastal erosion, e.g. deciding which parts of the coast should be protected, and how.

Further discussion suggestions

- Why do many major cities, such as London, Paris and Washington DC, have a by-pass that encircles the whole city?
- How would you decide on the route for a by-pass around your nearest town?
- Is building a by-pass likely to reduce passing trade in a town or village, or even destroy businesses altogether?

Answers to activities

1 a, b and c

Considerations	Red route	Blue route	Yellow route
Is the shortest route		✓	
Avoids all the built-up area	✓		
Avoids best farmland		✓	✓
Avoids steep slopes	✓	✓	
Avoids floodplain			✓
Avoids caravan park	✓		✓
Needs fewest bridges		✓	
Requires fewest trees to be cut down	✓		
Avoids new housing estate	✓		✓
Avoids sports park	✓	✓	
Total	6	5	4

Result The route with the most advantages (which pupils are encouraged to choose) is the red route.

2 a Pupils' descriptions of the red route should be similar to this:

The by-pass begins at ... the junction of the main road with a minor road. It passes to the right of a farm, crosses two minor roads and some of the best farmland. It runs across the floodplain and crosses the river and railway before rejoining the main road to Carlisle.

b Disadvantages (pupils need to give three): the fact that it is not the shortest route; it goes across some of the best farmland; crosses the floodplain and needs more bridges.

c Advantages (pupils need to give two but they should not gain credit for direct opposites): avoids the new housing estate; it avoids the steepest slope and requires fewer trees to be cut down.

3 a The walkers would not be happy with the blue route because the new road would go through farmland and require the cutting down of many trees.

b Walkers would be against the yellow route as it passes close to the Peelwell walk. Increased traffic and noise would disturb the peace and quiet that people enjoy when walking.

Residents of Peelwell would be against the yellow route as it would pass close to their houses. There would be an increase in noise levels and pollution from exhaust fumes, etc.

The hotel owner might be against the yellow route as it would take customers away from the town. (Note that this would be true for any route.)

4 Urbanisation

Pupil Book pages 70–71

The urbanisation enquiry

About this spread

The urbanisation enquiry is for the end of the Urbanisation unit, and provides an opportunity to assess pupils' progress. Also see the self-assessment checklist in Appendix 3 on page 62.

Learning outcomes

By the end of this spread pupils should be able to:

- interpret and use drawings to identify problems and solutions in an area
- complete two environmental quality surveys
- recommend whether or not the improvement scheme should go ahead.

What is the urbanisation enquiry about?

This enquiry builds on work done earlier in this unit, particularly on the problems of settlement growth and the problems of traffic in urban areas. The enquiry provides pupils with a drawing of a typical main street in a UK town that has problems of congestion, a lack of parking, buildings that are neglected and in a poor state of repair, and an unattractive environment with no landscaping. It also provides pupils with a drawing of a proposed improvement scheme for the area.

Pupils should begin the enquiry by identifying the problems that exist in the street and then look to see how the area could be improved under the suggested scheme. They complete an environmental quality survey for the street as it exists and under the proposed improvement scheme. They consider the views of local people and finally decide whether the improvement scheme should go ahead. They should write a letter to the local authority giving their views and suggestions.

How can enquiries help with assessment?

For each enquiry in *Foundations* there is a checklist in the appendices. The checklist provides pupils with success criteria so that they know what is expected in order to produce high-quality answers and improve in the future. The checklist can be used in two ways.

- Pupils can use these as they go along, to check that they are meeting the success criteria for the enquiry.
- They can be used for assessment either by you, as the teacher, or another pupil, for peer marking. Any element that is not ticked provides evidence that the pupil has not met all of the criteria.

Learning objectives

On this spread pupils should learn:

- how to use an environmental quality survey to measure the success of an urban improvement scheme
- that different people have different views that must be considered.

Differentiation suggestions

For lower-ability pupils

- Work with pupils to make sure they are clear about what they need to do and the stages they need to go through in the enquiry. You could suggest a maximum number of problems for them to find in diagram A.
- Provide pupils with a copy of the environmental quality survey sheet for the area before improvements, which is partially completed (see below). Omit the need for pupils to suggest further improvements for the area.
- Suggest to pupils that Mr Banks might not be in favour of the improvements because the street has been pedestrianised. Since he often has to drive to his shops in other towns, this could mean that it will take him longer. On the other hand, the proposed improvements might encourage more people to shop in this area, and his shop could benefit from this.

High quality	5	4	3	2	1	Low quality
Attractive				✓		Ugly
Quiet				✓		Noisy
Tidy					✓	Untidy
Safe					✓	Dangerous
Few cars						Many cars
Easy movement						Congested
Good shopping						Poor shopping
Good parking						Poor parking
Open space						No open space
Like						Dislike

Place *Drawing A – area before improvements*   Total _____ out of 50

For higher-ability pupils

There are a couple of possibilities.

- Give pupils the topic for enquiry, and the resources they need, but let them plan their own route through.
- Provide pupils with the enquiry in the pupil book and, once this is completed, provide them with similar data for another area, e.g. your local area, and ask them to complete a similar enquiry.

5 Kenya and Africa

Pupil Book pages 74–75

What are Africa's main physical features?

About this spread

On this spread pupils will learn about the location of the main rivers and mountains in Africa.

Learning outcomes

By the end of this spread pupils should be able to:
- name and locate Lake Victoria, the mouth of the Nile, the Cape of Good Hope, the Atlas mountains and the Victoria Falls
- use an atlas to give precise locations using of latitude and longitude.

Skills builder

Further practice is given in describing and interpreting photographs. In order to reinforce the understanding of latitude and longitude, you give the pupils the latitude and longitude of a city and get them to use their atlas to find the correct answer. Use could be made of other maps of Africa in the atlas such as thematic ones illustrating climate and vegetation.

Learning objectives

On this spread pupils should learn:
- how to make use of an atlas map of an enhanced satellite image
- to describe the main features shown on a photograph
- the names and locations of the main mountains and rivers in Africa
- about the main physical features of Africa.

Further discussion suggestions

- Pupils are asked to imagine they are going to spend a holiday journeying through Africa. They are to suggest three areas they would like to visit and to give their reasons why.
- Using the physical map of Africa pupils suggest why the centre of the continent remained unexplored for so long.

Answers to activities

1
  a 7400 kilometres
  b 6000 kilometres
  c Pupils should measure the rivers and rift valley as best they can. Because of the small scale of the map and the difficulties in measuring intricate lines, the answers will vary.
  Congo: approximately 2750 kilometres
  Zambezi: approximately 2500 kilometres
  d Rift Valley, eastern arm (to the most southerly point): approximately 3300 kilometres
  Rift Valley, western arm (to the join with the eastern arm): approximately 1500 kilometres

2

Location	Latitude	Longitude
Lake Victoria	0°	32°E
The mouth of the Nile	30°N	30°E
The Cape of Good Hope	34°S	18°E
The Atlas Mountains	30–35°N	1–10°W
Victoria Falls	18°S	24°E

3 Pupils' responses may vary, but should be along the following lines:

Earthquakes and volcanic activity The Great Rift Valley was formed by earth movements millions of years age. These earth movements are still taking place. Mount Kilimanjaro is an old volcano. Earthquakes were very common in East Africa.

Vegetation features The world's largest hot desert is the Sahara. The world's second largest forest is the Congo rainforest where there are thousands of different types of trees.

River features The Nile is nearly 7000 kilometres long and is the world's longest river. It flows north through ten different countries into the Mediterranean Sea. The largest waterfall in Africa is the Victoria Falls on the River Zambezi.

Wildlife There are large herds of lions, elephants, giraffes and zebras on the plains of East Africa. The Congo rain forest is full of wildlife and insects.

4 Pupils' responses may vary, but should be along the following lines:

Photo A In the foreground the landscape is flat and is covered with sand. The hills are very steep and there is no vegetation of any kind.

Photo B The Victoria Falls are formed as the river flows over the steep edge from a flat area in the background of the photo. This causes a great deal of spray. The river flows through a steep-sided valley which is crossed by a single span bridge. The sides of the valley are covered in vegetation.

Photo C People are riding elephants to cross the river. By the side of the river is grassland but there is also dense forest.

5 Kenya and Africa

Pupil Book pages 76–77

What are Africa's main human features?

About this spread

The pupils will learn about the main human features of Africa by referring to its growing population and low standard of living and quality of life of much of the population. There is recognition of the improvements in several countries due to economic growth. This has resulted in improved living conditions for many of the inhabitants.

Learning objectives

On this spread pupils should learn:

- the names and location of the countries of Africa
- the distribution of resources in Africa
- the human problems facing Africa.

Learning outcomes

By the end of this spread pupils should be able to:

- know the names of the largest and smallest countries in Africa
- locate countries that are rich in resources
- understand that there are great extremes of wealth and poverty in Africa
- name the problems the continent is still facing.

Skills builder

This spread starts to give pupils the opportunity to develop their sense of place. It also will allow them to appreciate that they must not develop a stereotypical view of Africa of it being poor and underdeveloped. They will recognise that although extreme poverty exists, there are parts of the continent which are well endowed with resources and that the cities, especially, have much in common with those in the UK and parts of Western Europe.

Key vocabulary

- **birth rate**
- **standard of living**
- **quality of life**

Further discussion suggestions

- What is the difference between standard of living and quality of life?
- How can some of the human problems in Africa be addressed?
- How can an African country rich in resources or with growing industry improve the living conditions of its inhabitants?

Answers to activities

1.

Location	Latitude	Longitude
Cairo	29°N	31°E
Nairobi	2°S	37°E
Cape Town	35°S	19°E
Dakar	15°N	17°W

2. a Ethiopia, South Sudan, Uganda and Tanzania
   b Namibia, Botswana, Lesotho, Swaziland and Mozambique
   c Algeria, Tunisia, Egypt, Sudan, Chad and Niger

3. Africa: human features

   Pupils' responses may vary, but should be along the following lines:

   Population The most densely populated areas are along the northern and western coasts and in the valleys of the rivers Nile, Niger and Congo. Cairo is the largest city in Africa with a population of over 17 million. Nigeria is the country with the largest population.

   Problems Poverty, illiteracy, malnutrition and inadequate water supplies affect a large proportion of the African population. Half the people in Central Africa live on less than £1 per day. More than 40% of the world's refugees come from Africa. They leave their homes because of wars, drought, famine and poverty.

   Industry and resources Africa is rich in minerals especially cobalt, platinum, chromium, coltan and gold. Angola, Libya and Nigeria have huge reserves of oil. Agriculture and mining are the main industries in Africa and there is a growing tourist industry.

   Signs of improvement Nigeria is expected to be one of the world's top economies by 2060.

4. Pupils' responses may vary, but should be along the following lines:

   Photo A Shows that there is a mixture of building types from large tower blocks to a minaret, which is part of a mosque. In the centre of the photograph there is a circular open space with roads radiating out from it. Many of the roads are full of traffic.

   Photo B Shows an open air market where the women in brightly-coloured dresses are putting out their fruit for sale. There are sunshades in the background showing that the climate is hot and sunny. There is also a covered part of the market in the background.

   Photo C A flat-topped mountain is in the background, which is surrounded by a layer of cloud. There are high rise buildings and warehouses in the background. In the foreground there are boats tied up at the dockside.

5 Kenya and Africa

Pupil Book pages 78–79

What are Kenya's main features?

About this spread

This spread introduces pupils to the idea that, while Kenya is a poor, developing country in terms of its income, it is rich in terms of its scenery and wildlife and has become a popular tourist destination. This spread encourages pupils to investigate Kenya's main features.

Learning objectives

On this spread pupils should learn:
- that Kenya is a developing country
- about the location of some of Kenya's main features.

Learning outcomes

By the end of this spread pupils should be able to:
- define the terms 'developing country', 'developed country' and 'standard of living'
- describe Kenya's location and some of its human and physical features.

Skills builder

This unit is about 'real' geography. It will be real to pupils because it is about actual people and real places. Pupils will learn how to apply their knowledge and understanding of geographical concepts to real places. When investigating places, pupils should consider where it is, what it is like, how it came to be like this, and how it might change.

Key vocabulary

- standard of living
- developing country
- developed country
- ethnic

Further discussion suggestions

- What are the differences between Nairobi and Mombasa in terms of their location, climate, economy and population?
- Why is neighbouring Somalia a perceived threat to Kenya's important tourism industry?
- How is Kenya's Maasai Mara National Reserve linked to the Serengeti National Park of Tanzania. What is the 'Great Migration'?

Answers to activities

1.
   a. A 'developing country' is one that is often quite poor, has few services and a low standard of living.
   b. A 'developed country' is one that has a lot of money, many services and a high standard of living.
   c. 'Standard of living' means how well-off a person or country is.
   d. 'Ethnic' means a group of people with common characteristics of race, nationality, language, religion or culture.

2.
   a. Somali Republic, Ethiopia, Sudan, Uganda, Tanzania
   b. Nakuru, Kisumu/Nairobi, Mombasa (Nakuru is the highest)
   c. Approximately 450 km
   d. Approximately 800 km
   e. Approximately 900 km

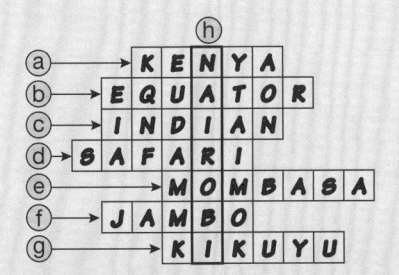

3.
   a. KENYA
   b. EQUATOR
   c. INDIAN
   d. SAFARI
   e. MOMBASA
   f. JAMBO
   g. KIKUYU

   Pupils' clues for the down-word (h) should relate to the fact that Nairobi is Kenya's capital and one of its major cities.

4. Pupils should describe Kenya using the information from pages 78–79 of the pupil book.

5 Kenya and Africa

Pupil Book pages 80–81

What are Kenya's main physical features?

About this spread

This spread follows on directly from 'What are Kenya's main features?' by focusing on Kenya's main physical features: landforms, vegetation and climate. Kenya lies on the Equator, so average temperatures are high throughout the year, but rainfall varies. The climate is not the same across the country. The north is hot and dry. Further south and along the coast temperatures are high, but there is more rainfall. In Nairobi temperatures are lower than on the coast as the city is 1820 metres above sea level.

Learning outcomes

By the end of this spread pupils should be able to:

- explain how the Great Rift Valley was formed
- describe and explain Mount Kenya's main features
- describe Nairobi's climate.

Key vocabulary

- volcanic activity
- rift valley

Learning objectives

On this spread pupils should learn:

- about some of Kenya's main physical features: its landforms, vegetation and climate.

Skills builder

One of the skills that pupils need to develop in geography is the ability to use and interpret a wide range of graphs and diagrams. They need to be able to draw them, and interpret what they show. This spread provides pupils with practice in interpreting an annotated drawing of Kenya showing its physical features (drawing B) and climate graphs for Nairobi and Mombasa. In Activity 1, pupils also use a diagram to explain how the Great Rift Valley was formed.

If you want to give your pupils some practice at drawing climate graphs, you could give temperature and rainfall figures for Mombasa to enable pupils to draw their own climate graph.

Further discussion suggestions

- How did shield volcanoes form in Kenya's Great Rift Valley?
- Describe the appearance and wildlife of the Kenyan savanna.
- How does Lake Turkana differ from Lake Victoria?

Answers to activities

1. **a** The Great Rift Valley is a wide, deep, steep-sided valley that runs almost the whole length of Africa.

   b

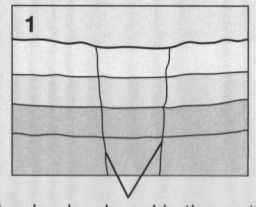

   1 Cracks developed in the earth when the Central Highlands was an area of volcanic activity, millions of years ago.

   2 Over 60 km wide in places. Land between the cracks collapsed, creating the Great Rift Valley. It has steep sides and is very deep and long.

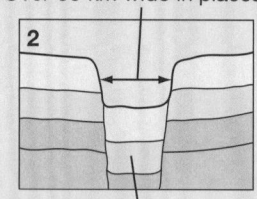

2. Pupils' captions for photo A should both describe and explain the mountain's main features. The caption should be along the following lines (words from the textbox should be included and are shown in bold).

   Mount Kenya is an old **cone-shaped volcano** with **steep, rocky** slopes. It is **5,899 m high** and is Kenya's highest mountain. The fact that it is so high means that it stays **cold** and **snow-covered** all year, even though it is on the **Equator**.

3. **a** March, April and May.

   b Approximately 20 mm.

   c 16 °C

   d Nairobi is cooler than Mombasa because it is higher above sea level; temperature decreases with height.

4. **a** Pupils' descriptions will vary, but they should use the headings provided (shown in bold below) and some of the following information.

   General weather Temperatures are high throughout the year with plenty of sunshine. There is rainfall throughout the year, with more in April and May. Sea breezes cool the coast in the afternoon, but evenings are warm and pleasant.

   July temperature 24 °C

   July rainfall Approximately 80 mm.

   Coastal landforms The coast has long sandy beaches, with coral reefs offshore.

   Vegetation cover Tropical rainforest runs along the coast, with lush green vegetation.

   Sea conditions The Indian Ocean is warm and clear.

   b April and May are the worst months to take a holiday in the area as this is the rainy season. In May, rainfall can measure 250 mm, which is nearly one-fifth of the year's total rainfall.

5 Kenya and Africa

Pupil Book pages 82–83

Why is Kenya's population unevenly spread/ Present-day movements of population

About this spread

This spread looks at Kenya's population distribution and links to Chapter 3 Population in *Nelson Key Geography Connections*. Page 82 shows how early movements of people into Kenya were from different directions and how different groups then settled in very different physical areas: the semi-desert in the north, the grasslands in the south-west, the highlands of the centre and towards the east, and the coastal area. Page 83 looks at present-day movements and gives reasons as to why the Kikuyu in particular are moving from their rural environment to the capital city of Nairobi.

Learning outcomes

By the end of this spread pupils should be able to:

- describe how the distribution of population in Kenya is mainly affected by physical factors
- give reasons why people leave rural villages in Kenya
- list the advantages of living in the capital city, Nairobi.

Key vocabulary

- migration
- rural-to-urban migration

Learning objectives

On this spread pupils should learn:

- about the physical factors that have affected Kenya's population distribution
- about the migration of people in Kenya today.

Skills builder

Understanding distributions and patterns is a key geographical skill. This spread explains that Kenya's population, as in many other countries, is not evenly distributed. Some areas are more densely populated, while other areas are sparsely populated. Page 82 of the pupil book will help pupils to understand the reasons behind this distribution, which relates to migration (where people originally came from) and physical factors (how climate and relief affected where people settled).

Further discussion suggestions

- What factors affect where people live?
- Does most of Kenya's population live in towns and cities, or in the countryside?

Answers to activities

1.
   - Kenya's population is not spread evenly.
   - The Maasai came from the Nile Valley and live in the south-west.
   - The Kikuyu came from the south and west and live on higher land.
   - Arabs and Indians tend to live on the coast near Mombasa.

2.

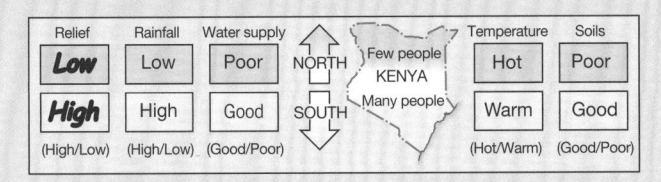

Relief	Rainfall	Water supply		Temperature	Soils
Low	Low	Poor	NORTH — Few people KENYA	Hot	Poor
High	High	Good	SOUTH — Many people	Warm	Good
(High/Low)	(High/Low)	(Good/Poor)		(Hot/Warm)	(Good/Poor)

3. a) Reasons for leaving the village include: there are too many people to find jobs on the farms and in the shambas; the skills people learned at school cannot be used in the local villages; many of the people are farmers and either only own small plots of land, or no land at all.

   b) Nairobi has hospitals, shops, cinemas and a university; it will be easy for people to adapt to city life as they have lived in villages and small towns for a long time; people can live in Nairobi and still get back to visit their villages as it is not too far to travel.

5 Kenya and Africa

Pupil Book pages 84–85

What is it like living in Nairobi?

About this spread

This spread looks at what migrants to Nairobi might find when they arrive in the city. While Nairobi has a more affluent city centre, most migrants live and work on the outskirts of the city in one of the shanty settlements. Settlements like Kibera are found in many of the world's poorer countries. They often develop on poor quality land, they are usually overcrowded with shelters made from any material that is available, and there is often no proper sanitation. Kibera is no exception.

Learning outcomes

By the end of this spread pupils should be able to:

- understand that cities in developing countries may have wealthy city centres, and shanty settlements where most migrants live
- describe the problems of living in a shanty settlement
- list the good points about living in Nairobi.

Key vocabulary

- shanty settlement
- sewage

Learning objectives

On this spread pupils should learn:

- that Nairobi has a wealthy city centre, but that most migrants live in shanty settlements like Kibera
- about the problems associated with living in Kibera.

Skills builder

This spread includes five different photos – four of shanty settlements around Nairobi and one of Nairobi city centre. They provide a great opportunity for pupils to really analyse what they show. Encourage pupils to think deeply about the photos. Some questions you could ask and they could think about include the following:

- What do these photos show?
- Could other photos have been chosen instead?
- What is life like for the people shown in the photos?
- How might life change for the people?
- What could happen to make it change?
- How would pupils feel if they lived there?

Further discussion suggestions

- What attracts people from rural parts of Kenya to Nairobi?
- How can life in shanty settlements, like Kibera, be improved?

Answers to activities

1. Pupils are asked for three differences between photos A and B. They may come up with others, but the following are some of the more obvious differences.

   Photo A shows tall, modern buildings; photo B shows low, poorly built housing.

   Photo A has tree-lined, paved streets; photo B has unpaved, cluttered streets.

   Photo A is quiet with wide-open spaces; photo B is crowded with narrow streets.

2. a 6 km

   b Kibera is south-west of the city centre.

   c The correct words are shown in bold in the following sentence.

   Shanty settlements are areas of **poor quality** housing found at the **edge** of the city on **poor quality** building land.

3. Pupils are asked for four problems of life in a shanty settlement. They include: open sewers (this is a health hazard, and in the rainy season sewage in the streets makes the tracks unusable); poor quality housing (made from mud, corrugated iron, and so on); houses are close together with little space between them; few services such as clean water or electricity.

4. Pupils are asked for four ways that people in a shanty settlement can earn money. They include: selling food from stalls; running shops such as hairdressers and battery-charging businesses from their homes; collecting waste material and recycling it in small workshops.

5. a Good points about living in Nairobi include: migrants may already have family and friends in Nairobi; migrants can move in with family and friends; migrants can share food and jobs with family and friends; migrants may eventually be able to build their own home in a shanty settlement.

   b One side of Nairobi is the city centre with its pleasant environment and modern buildings. Richer people live and work in good conditions in or near the city centre. The other side of Nairobi is where poorer people live and work, in shanty settlements a long way from the city centre on the outskirts of the city.

5 Kenya and Africa

Pupil Book pages 86–87

What is the Maasai way of life?

About this spread

This spread looks at the life of one of Kenya's ethnic groups, the Maasai. Their lives revolve around the fact that they are pastoralists, and some are nomadic. This spread looks at how the landscape, weather and wealth affect the housing, dress, daily life and diet of traditional Maasai.

Learning objectives

On this spread pupils should learn:

- about the lifestyle, housing and dress of one of Kenya's ethnic groups.

Learning outcomes

By the end of this spread pupils should be able to:

- describe how the landscape, weather and wealth affect the family life, housing, clothing and diet of the Maasai.

Key vocabulary

- pastoralists
- diet

Skills builder

This spread will encourage pupils to see how other people's lives differ from their own. Their study of the Maasai way of life will open their eyes to the fact that all over the world people have values and attitudes that are different from their own. For the Maasai, cattle are hugely important. They depend on cattle for food, and use their skins for bedding and dung for building. The Maasai's wealth is measured not in terms of money, but by cattle. The material on this spread will encourage pupils to think about their own values and attitudes, and to empathise with people from different cultures.

Further discussion suggestions

- Which lifestyle would you prefer – the life of the Maasai, or someone living in Kibera?
- In what ways have many Maasai moved away from their traditional lifestyle?
- Maasai wealth is measured by number of children as well as cattle. Why is this?

Answers to activities

1. a Pupils are asked for two facts about a developing country. These could include the fact that a developing country: is often quite poor; has few services; has a low standard of living.

   b An ethnic group is a group of people with common characteristics of race, nationality, language, religion or culture.

   c Africa

2. a The Maasai depend on the cattle for their food (a major part of their diet is milk mixed with blood from their cows). Cattle, not money, represent wealth to the Maasai.

   b Pupils' paragraphs should include the words in the textbox (shown in bold below). Their paragraphs should be along the following lines. The area where the Maasai live and farm consists of **flat land**. The Maasai keep herds of **cattle and goats** and some are **nomadic**. This means they move about to find water and **grass** for their animals. The grass needs **rain** to grow, and the rainy seasons are between April and June, and October to November.

3.
   1 The roof is made of grass
   2 The hut is 4 m wide and 4 m long
   3 The hut is only about the height of an adult
   4 The door is narrow with an arch shape – it leads to a small tunnel entrance
   5 The walls are made from mud from nearby rivers, and cow dung
   6 This opening is needed for ventilation (fresh air) as there are no windows or chimney

4. a The people in photo A are wearing relatively light clothes and have bare legs. The hut has no windows, which suggests that people do not spend much time inside. The lack of windows also means it stays cool. The clothing and design of the hut suggest that the weather is usually warm.

   b The walls are made from mud and cow dung. If the weather was very wet, they would simply disintegrate.

5 Kenya and Africa

Pupil Book pages 88–89

What is a developing country?

About this spread

This spread looks at a variety of criteria (or indicators) that are often used to investigate differences in the levels of development between different countries. It looks in general terms at what a developing country is, and could be used for other countries as well as Kenya. Development is often measured in terms of wealth. On this spread, wealth is defined as gross national product (GNP). GNP is given in US dollars to allow comparisons to be made between countries. Other ways of measuring development that are often used are given in table B.

Learning outcomes

By the end of this spread pupils should be able to:
- describe the different ways of measuring the level of development of a country
- describe developing countries in terms of their GNP, trade, population, health and education
- describe the global distribution of richer and poorer countries.

Key vocabulary

- developing country
- developed country
- standard of living
- gross national product (GNP)
- birth rate
- population growth
- death rate
- infant mortality
- life expectancy
- health
- literacy rate

Learning objectives

On this spread pupils should learn:
- about how we measure a country's level of development
- about the global distribution of rich and poor countries.

Skills builder

Ask pupils to compare Kenya and the UK in terms of adult literacy rates, life expectancy, GDP, etc. This will provide practice in using the internet for research purposes. Pupils need to use and find information from a variety of sources and, increasingly, will be accessing information online. Using the internet to find the information we want can be quick and rewarding, or slow and frustrating. Help pupils as much as you can by ensuring that when searching for information:

- they are asking the right questions, and searching for the right information
- know where to find information and which websites can be trusted and which are best avoided (suggest websites for pupils to use whenever possible), and are aware of when they are getting side-tracked, or going down blind alleys.

Further discussion suggestions

- Why will using just one measure to decide how developed a country is often not gives a true picture?
- As a country becomes more developed what is likely to happen to its birth rate and literacy rate?
- A country's natural increase of population is the difference between its birth rate and death rate. Use an atlas to work out the population natural increase of a range of countries at different stages of development.

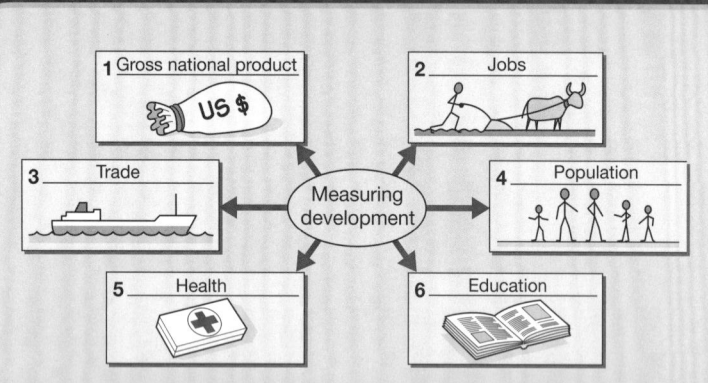

Answers to activities

1

- 1 Gross national product (US $)
- 2 Jobs
- 3 Trade
- 4 Population
- 5 Health
- 6 Education

(all linked to central "Measuring development")

2

Developing countries	Developed countries
Poor countries	Rich countries
Small GNP	Large GNP
Little trade	A lot of trade
Poor education and poor health care	Good education and health care
High infant mortality	Low infant mortality
Rapid population growth	Slow population growth
Low literacy rate	High literacy rate
High birth and death rates	Low birth and death rates
Kenya and Egypt	Japan, USA and UK
Africa, South America and South-east Asia	Europe, North America and Australasia
The South	The North

5 Kenya and Africa

Pupil Book pages 90–91

The Kenya enquiry

About this spread

The Kenya enquiry is intended to be used at the end of the Kenya unit. It is one of four enquiries in the pupil book, and provides an opportunity to assess pupils' progress. Note that you might want to update the figures in diagram C on page 91. You could use the CIA World Factbook to find most of the information. Also see the self-assessment checklist in Appendix 4 on page 64.

What is the Kenya enquiry about?

Pupils have learned in this unit that Kenya is, in terms of its wealth, a poor country. It is very different to the UK. In this enquiry, pupils imagine that they work for a department of the British government responsible for overseas development and have been asked to produce a report on Kenya's level of development. The report should consist of four parts describing:

- how developed Kenya is compared with the UK
- how developed Kenya is compared with neighbouring countries in Africa
- how developed Kenya is in terms of social and cultural measures of development
- in which areas of development Kenya is in greatest need of improvement, with suggestions about what might be done to help Kenya make progress.

Before they can write their report, pupils need to complete a table by ranking development measures for different countries.

Learning outcomes

By the end of this spread pupils should be able to:

- understand how different indicators can be used to measure development
- rank different countries according to development indicators
- produce a report to assess Kenya's level of development and identify areas for improvement.

How can enquiries help with assessment?

For each enquiry in the pupil book, there is a checklist supplied in the appendices. The checklist provides pupils with success criteria so that they know what is expected in order to produce high-quality answers and improve in the future. The checklist can be used in two ways.

- Pupils can use these as they go along, to check that they are meeting the success criteria for the enquiry.
- They can be used for assessment, either by you, as the teacher, or another pupil (for peer marking). Any element that is not ticked provides evidence that the pupil has not met all the criteria.

Differentiation suggestions

For lower-ability pupils

Work with pupils to make sure they are clear about the steps they need to go through in order to complete the enquiry.

- Recap the work done on pages 88–89 of the pupil book on how to measure development.
- Ensure pupils are clear about what the different development indicators mean.
- Check that pupils know how to rank the indicators and work through one with them.
- Provide a writing frame for pupils to use to complete their report.

For higher-ability pupils

- Ask higher-ability pupils to include the terms 'standard of living', 'quality of life' and 'sustainable development' in their reports.

6 Ordnance Survey maps

Pupil Book pages 92–93

How can we show direction?

About this spread

This spread begins by explaining what maps are and why they are useful to geographers. The main aim of the spread is to show how to give direction. The eight-point compass is used and the emphasis is on simple and interesting activities to teach direction. At this level, it is helpful to use the words 'from' and 'to' whenever giving directions.

Learning objectives

On this spread pupils should learn:
- how to show direction using the points of the compass
- that there are four main points of the compass (N, S, E, W), with a further four points between them (N-E, S-E, S-W, N-W).

Learning outcomes

By the end of this spread pupils should be able to:
- understand that maps are a good way of providing information and showing where places are
- give directions using the points of a compass.

Key vocabulary

- map
- Ordnance Survey
- plan
- direction
- compass points

Skills builder

For all pupils
- Check their understanding as they go through the spread.
- Show them examples of maps that have North Points marked on them – many of the maps in the pupil book do, e.g. page 27D, page 45D, page 78A. Note that world maps generally do not have a North Point, as it is understood the top edge of the map will be north.
- Introduce pupils to using real compasses.

For higher-ability pupils
- Use Activity 5 on page 93 with these pupils (giving directions using the OS map of the Cambridge area on the inside back cover).
- Ask them to write instructions for Year 6 pupils to explain how to give directions.
- Ask pupils to work in pairs, each one working out a route on the OS map of Cambridge on the inside back cover using compass directions. The other person has to follow the route.

Further discussion suggestions

- What is the Ordnance Survey (use the internet to find out)?
- How would you use a map in orienteering?
- Walking from home to school, how many times would you change direction and what points of the compass would you follow? (Use a local A–Z street map to work it out).

Answers to activities

1

(Eight-point compass rose showing North, North-east, East, South-east, South, South-west, West, North-west)

2
- B is north of A.
- D is north-west of C.
- F is south-west of E.
- H is south-east of G.
- I is west of J.

3
a East
b North-east
c North-west
d North-west
e South

4 a Leave Port A
Go east to point 1
Go south-east to point 2
Go east to point 3
Go north-east to point 4
Go east to point 5
Go south to point 6
Go west to point 7
Go south-west to point 8
Go north-west to point 9
Go west to point 10
Go south-west to Port B

b Leave Port B
Go north-east to point 10
Go north-east to point 2
Go north-west to point 1
Go west to Port A

5
a East
b North-east
c South
d West
e South-east

6 Ordnance Survey maps

Pupil Book pages 94–95

How can we measure distance?

About this spread

This spread is concerned with measuring distance. A straightforward method is explained using the edge of a piece of paper. Pupils should be encouraged to state the units they are measuring in, and to be accurate when measuring. Activities could include measuring distances around the school using a school plan.

Learning outcomes

By the end of this spread pupils should be able to:
- understand that distances on a map can be measured using the scale line
- measure distances between places on maps using the scale line.

Key vocabulary

- scale

Further discussion suggestions

- How far away is your home from school 'as the crow flies'?
- What does this mean?
- Using a 1 : 50,000 map of the area, what is the approximate walking distance between your home and your school?
- Which of these map scales would show greater detail on a map: 1 : 50,000, 1 : 25,000 or 1 : 10,000?

Learning objectives

On this spread pupils should learn:
- about the concept of scale, and how it is shown on a map
- how to measure distances on a map using the scale line.

Skills builder

Use the OS map on the inside back cover of the pupil book. Ask them to work out both the straight line distance and the distance on the ground between the places in the table below. Tell them to use the kilometre scale line opposite the map. The animation available on Kerboodle will assist them.

In order to complete this activity, pupils will need to know that:
- stations are shown by red dots
- motorways are in blue, and the junctions are numbered.

Lower-ability pupils may find it easier to work on a 1 : 25,000 scale Ordnance Survey map extract.

	Straight line distance	Actual distance
From Foxton station to Great Shelford station		
From junction 11 to junction 13 on the motorway		
From Cantelupe Farm (grid square 4254) to Rectory Farm (grid square 4252)		

Answers to activities

1.
   a. Line a is 40 metres (m) in length.
   b. Line b is 100 metres (m) in length.
   c. Line c is 60 metres (m) in length.
   d. Line d is 90 metres (m) in length.

2.
   a. 80 m
   b. 40 m
   c. 120 m
   d. 100 m

3.
   a. 140 m
   b. 240 m

4. 220 m

5. In the hills
   Under the bridge
   Correct answer is: Below the big tree

6 Ordnance Survey maps

Pupil Book pages 96–97

What are grid references?

About this spread

This spread explains what grid references are, how to give a four-figure grid reference, and how to find a four-figure grid reference. Pupils can easily get confused with grid references, so a very simple approach is used here, with a minimum of text.

Learning objectives

On this spread pupils should learn:

- what grid references are
- how to use four-figure grid references.

Learning outcomes

By the end of this spread pupils should be able to:

- understand that grid references can be used to help describe the location of a place on a map
- locate a grid square on a map using a four-figure grid reference
- give four-figure grid references.

Skills builder

Pupils could work in pairs using the OS map extract on the inside back cover of the pupil book or a different OS map. One pupil describes the route of a journey across the map using only grid references, which the other pupil has to follow. They then swap around. Compass directions could also be included in order to revise this additional skill.

Key vocabulary

- grid square
- four-figure grid references

Further discussion suggestions

- What size are the grid squares on a 1 : 25,000 OS map and a 1 : 50,000 OS map?
- What does 'eastings before northings' mean?
- What is the National Grid Reference System?

Answers to activities

1.
   a Manchester
   b Glasgow
   c Bristol
   d Belfast
2.
   a Grampian Mountains
   b Southern Uplands
   c Pennines
3.
   a The Rivers Severn, Trent and Thames
   b The River Severn
4.
   a 0002
   b 0203
   c 0300
   d 0102
5. Pupils need to be able to locate the place where they live on map C, and then give the correct four-figure grid reference for it.
6.
   a Manor Farm
   b Haggis Farm
   c River Farm
   d Rectory Farm
   e Laundry Farm

6 Ordnance Survey maps

How do we use six-figure grid references?

Pupil Book pages 98–99

About this spread

This spread explains that in order to locate a place accurately on a map, we need to use a six-figure grid reference rather than a four-figure grid reference. The activities provide pupils with practice in finding places using six-figure grid references, and in giving six-figure grid references. As with the previous spread, a very simple approach is used here with a minimum of text.

Learning outcomes

By the end of this spread pupils should be able to:
- locate features on a map using six-figure grid references
- give six-figure grid references.

Key vocabulary

- six-figure grid reference
- symbol

Learning objectives

On this spread pupils should learn:
- how to use six-figure grid references.

Skills builder

As six-figure grid references refer to a specific point on the OS map extract, the opportunity could be used to make the pupils familiar with the key and the different map symbols. They can be asked to draw a map from a written description using appropriate symbols in order to test their knowledge and understanding of map symbols. An island will work particularly well. Pupils could also name local features and recognize the symbols on a map.

Further discussion suggestions

- Why are six-figure grid references more useful to the emergency services, such as mountain rescue and air-sea rescue than four-figure grid reference?
- What scales are OS Landranger and OS Explorer maps?
- Why do grid references sometimes have two letters in front, e.g. NZ 342 254, and how can this help when giving a grid reference for a distant UK location?

Answers to activities

1.
   a At 168245 there is a farm.
   b At 165257 there is a bridge.
   c At 175233 there is a level crossing.
   d At 177244 there is a roundabout.

2.
   a 163236
   b 178241
   c 165254
   d 178257

3.
   a Pupils need to follow the directions given.
   b The walk finishes at the bridge. The six-figure grid reference is 165257.
   c The most likely choice of place to stop for lunch would be the picnic site in Burr Wood.
   d The walk passes two churches at 175242 and 175246.

4. a and b

Symbol	Meaning	Six-figure grid reference
	Railway station	465523
	Motorway junction	440534
	Wood	488505
	Church with tower	418509
	Camp/caravan site	453539

6 Ordnance Survey maps

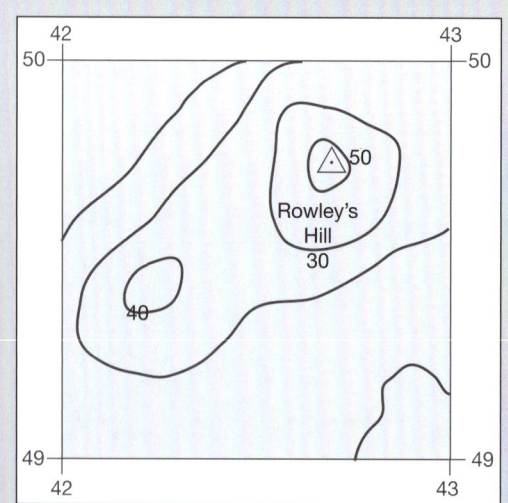

Pupil Book pages 100–101

How is height shown on a map?

About this spread

This spread explains what relief is (the shape of the land), and that map makers have to find ways of showing relief and height on maps. This spread looks at how height is shown on a map using spot heights, layer colouring and contours. Pages 102 and 103 explain in more detail how contours can be used to show height and relief.

Learning objectives

On this spread pupils should learn:

- that height can be shown on a map using different methods.

Learning outcomes

By the end of this spread pupils should be able to:

- understand that height is shown on maps using spot heights, layer colouring and contours
- understand the differences between spot heights, layer colouring and contours
- interpret maps using spot heights, layer colouring and contours.

Key vocabulary

- height
- relief
- spot height
- contour
- layer colouring (layer shading)

Skills builder

Get the pupils to start asking geographical questions which will allow them to describe the shape of the land in greater detail. For example:

- what is the highest point?
- what is the average height?
- how steep are the slopes of the hills?

Further discussion suggestions

- Explain the difference between relief and height
- Where would you usually find a triangulation pillar, and why?
- Must contours always be 'closed' (even if not fully shown on a map)?

Answers to activities

1 a Downward

C	O	N	T	O	U	R	S				
	S	P	O	T	H	E	I	G	H	T	
				S	L	O	P	E			
			H	E	I	G	H	T			
	L	A	Y	E	R	C	O	L	O	U	R	I	N	G
				F	L	A	T				

b Relief is used to describe the shape of the land, e.g. steeply sloping, gently sloping, flat, etc.

2 a G, B and F

b A and D

c C and E

3 a The land is shaded brown. The mountains are shown by red triangles.

b Over 500 metres

c The Cotswolds are between 100 and 500 metres high. The Chilterns are between 100 and 200 metres high.

d Pupils need to be able to locate their area on the map and read the height from the map.

4 a Grid square 4852: 30 m, 40 m, 50 m. Grid square 4450: 20 m, 30 m, 40 m

b Grid square 4151: 14 m. Grid square 4754: 18 m

c Grid square 4051: 61 m

5

6 Ordnance Survey maps

Pupil Book pages 102–103

How do contours show height and relief?

About this spread

This spread reminds pupils of what contours are and how they can be used to show the height of the land as well as its relief (shape). Contours drawn on a map can make up different patterns and these can help us to recognise different landscape features. The activities provide practice for pupils in interpreting height information from contours, recognising landscape features from contours, and drawing contour patterns for different landscape features.

Learning outcomes

By the end of this spread pupils should be able to:

- understand that contour lines are used to show height and relief on maps
- draw simple contour patterns for different landscape features
- recognise landforms from contour patterns.

Key vocabulary

- contours
- relief
- contour interval

Learning objectives

On this spread pupils should learn:

- that contours can be used to show height
- that the patterns contours make can tell us about the relief of the land.

Skills builder

Introduce terms for different relief features such as 'hill', 'valley' or 'plateau'. Use areas of different relief to show pupils that the closer together the contour lines on the map are, the steeper the slope on the earth's surface. Pupils should be taught that the accurate heights of a location can only be worked if it lies directly on a contour line or has a spot height figure next to it. Locations between contours can only be given as a range between the values of the adjacent contour lines.

Further discussion suggestions

- How can shading make relief stand out more on a contour map?
- How would you recognise a high cliff on a contour map?
- How might fell walkers in the Lake District find contours on a map useful?

Answers to activities

1
- a The highest point is 52 metres
- b Place E is 30 metres
- c Place B is 34 metres
- d Place A is 6 metres
- e Place D is 12 metres

3 a and b

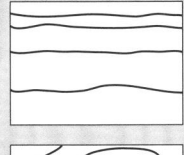

Gentle slope, with land rising in the distance.

This is a cone-shaped mountain with steep sides.

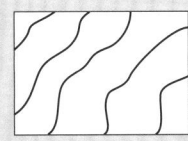

This is a winding valley, with gently-sloping sides and a stream.

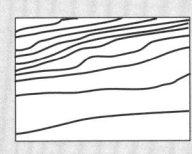

This is a steep-sided valley with a flat valley floor.

2
- a TRUE
- b FALSE
- c TRUE
- d TRUE
- e TRUE

4
1. A gentle slope **C**
2. A steep slope **D**
3. A hill top **E**
4. A flat valley floor **A**
5. A valley with a stream **F**
6. A valley without a stream **B**

7 Key skills: writing and photos

Pupil Book pages 104–105

How can we use key questions?

About this spread

This spread introduces pupils to the enquiry approach which is fundamental for developing a real understanding of the subject. It gives the opportunity for the pupils to be totally involved in their learning. It shows that pupils are required to describe and interpret written and pictorial information through the use of key geographical questions. It is shown that questions can be used to develop knowledge, understanding attitudes and values. At the same time they can be used to structure written work and so develop pupils' literacy skills.

Learning outcomes

By the end of this spread pupils should be able to:

- devise and use questions to describe geographical features, understand their formation and be able to have a personal view as well as appreciating the views of others on geographical matters
- use questions to structure written work in order to improve their literacy skills.

Key vocabulary

- key questions

Learning objectives

On this spread pupils should learn:

- that learning in geography is best achieved by asking questions
- that there are different types of questions
- that questions can be used when studying text and pictures.

Skills builder

Pupils should be given frequent opportunities to engage with written text and photos and to devise their own questions in order to improve their knowledge and understanding. They should be confronted by as much open verbal questioning in the lesson as possible in order for them to appreciate the type of questions most successful in extracting information.

Further discussion activities

- Which type of questions is most useful – closed or open?
- What is the difference between attitudes and values?
- What is the best way to use questions to structure a piece of geographical writing?

Answers to activities

1. Key questions are important geographical questions which describe or explain geographical features. They also can be used to express a personal view on a geographical issue and to express the opinions of other people or interested groups.

2. Scarborough is a small town in **North Yorkshire**. It is situated on the coast next to sandy **beaches** and a steep-sided **headland**. The original town grew up around the castle, which had a good **defensive** site. The **sheltered** harbour and good fishing helped the town develop in later years. Nowadays, Scarborough has become an important tourist **resort**. This has made it more crowded but has provided jobs and new amenities which the local people can use. Scarborough has an **attractive** location and plenty of things for **visitors** to do.

3. This landslide is on the coast. Material has slipped down as the cliff has collapsed and flowed out onto the beach. It collapsed because the rock became unstable after heavy rain or a storm. It has left a kind of valley and some buildings in the background have collapsed. This means that the area around the landslide is unsafe and dangerous. People may no longer be able to use the beach. It has given a new shape to the landscape. People who used the buildings may not be able to live or work there anymore. I think it is very impressive and shows how effective physical forces can be in changing the shape of the landscape.

4. **a** and **b**

- **What or where is it?** It shows a tree that has been blown over by a storm and has fallen across the road towards some shops.
- **What is it like?** It has broken up the pavement and blocked the road. It only just missed damaging the shops.
- **Why is it like that?** The wind was so strong that the tree was blown over. The roots pushed up the paving stones as it fell over.
- **How is it changing?** The road side would have lost one of its trees which had given the built-up area some greenery making it less attractive.
- **What have been the effects of these changes?** The area may not be as pleasant to live and work in as it used to be. The trees could have provided shelter to people walking along the pavement.
- **What do you think and feel about the place?** The storm had a bad effect on the place as it will become less attractive because there is less greenery. The tree should be replanted as soon as possible.

7 Key skills: writing and photos

Pupil Book pages 106–107

How can we describe places?

About this spread

In this spread pupils are given opportunities to engage fully with a photograph, to describe what they see and to use the information to infer some possible consequences of the factors described. The pupils are shown how to think geographically by relating the information directly to key geographical terms which can be physical, human or environmental.

Learning objectives

On this spread pupils should learn:

- to describe the physical and human features on a photograph in detail
- to make logical inferences of the effects of the factors described.

Learning outcomes

By the end of this spread pupils should be able to:

- write geographically by making use of geographical terms in their descriptions of photographs
- to increase their understanding of the effect of physical and human factors on the landscape and the local people.

Skills builder

The pupils will be provided with a list of geographical terms to help them to extract all the information from a particular photograph. It will allow them to appreciate that geography is a visual subject and that landscapes can be very complex. Opportunities should be given to compare the landscape on the photograph with a more familiar one in order to recognise differences and similarities. It will help them to appreciate that geography is about real places and real people.

Key vocabulary

- relief
- drainage
- climate
- population
- communications
- settlement

Further discussion activities

- Would you like to live in a place that that shown on the photograph?
- How could the conditions of the people living in the area shown on the photograph be improved?
- How might the landscape shown on the photograph change in the future?

Answers to activities

1.
   - The location is Boscastle in **North Cornwall**.
   - The relief is a **steep**-sided narrow **valley**.
   - The drainage is by the **river** flowing through Boscastle.
   - The climate seems to be **wet** as the river is flooding.
   - The vegetation is **woodland** and rough **moorland**.
   - There is a small **village** in the river valley.
   - Travel is difficult with only a narrow, winding **road** visible.
   - Many people may work in the **tourist** industry.
   - The floods had a great impact on Boscastle because the water has flooded the road and the village. This would have meant people found it difficult to get out and also the tourist industry would have suffered because so much was destroyed and the village became difficult to reach.

2. **Population** This is a crowded place because there are many people in the photograph which implies a high population. Many of them come from an ethnic minority.

   Settlement It is a built-up area but it is a poor area as some of the buildings are in need of repair.

   Communications The road is busy because there is a great deal of traffic passing through the area.

   Work/employment The people can work in the shops but the people shown walking or waiting in the street may be unemployed.

   Conclusion This seems to be a poor area of London where there may be many problems linked to a large number of people using inadequate and run-down facilities.

7 Key skills: writing and photos

Pupil Book pages 108–109

What are key words and key sentences?

About this spread

This spread is concerned with training pupils to get the most out of a text. This is done by identifying key words and key questions so that copying out irrelevant material is avoided. It is also a way for them to undertake revision effectively using their notes taken during the course.

Learning objectives

On this spread pupils should learn:

- to gain the maximum use of information from written sources
- how to annotate diagrams with the most meaningful information.

Learning outcomes

By the end of this spread pupils should be able to:

- separate irrelevant material in a written text from the key words and sentences
- read a piece of text with sufficient understanding to be able to identify the most important facts and information.

Key vocabulary

- key words
- key sentences

Skills builder

This spread will contribute greatly to developing and extending the pupils' literary proficiency. It will develop their ability to read and extract information in a meaningful manner. This should be a transferable skill because, when it is mastered, it should impact on the quality of their written communication. Their writing should become more concise and show an ability to come to a conclusion more easily without masses of irrelevant or unnecessary material.

Further discussion activities

- What are the key words and sentences in a newspaper article describing a local topical issue?
- What are the key words and sentences in a case study that can be identified and used to illustrate a more abstract geographical concept?

Answers to activities

1 **a, b** and **c**

- overflows its banks
- more water than it can hold
- floodplain (the flat area next to the river)
- heavy rain
- long period of time
- melting snow or ice
- always flooded
- natural causes (physical or not human causes)
- steep valley slopes
- impermeable rocks or soils (rocks or soils that do not allow water to pass through e.g. clay)
- very wet soil
- Floods are more common now
- human activity
- cutting down trees (deforestation)
- building more towns and cities (urbanisation)

2 **a** and **b**

Pupils need to make a copy of diagram D adding the following labels:

Natural causes

- If soil is full of water, no more rain can soak into it.
- Impermeable rocks and soils do not allow water to soak in.
- Water flows quickly down steep slopes. Little soaks in.

Human activity

- Cutting down trees increases the risk of flooding.
- Water flows across concrete and tarmac quickly to the river.
- Gutters and drains carry water directly to the river.

7 Key skills: writing and photos

Pupil Book pages 110–111

How can we describe physical features on a photograph?

About this spread

This spread shows how pupils can identify and describe the main physical features shown on a photograph. This will enable them to appreciate the nature of the landscape, making use of descriptive writing, either in continuous prose or by adding annotations. The activities provide practice for pupils in using correct geographical terms and referring to specific points of detail on the photograph.

Learning objectives

On this spread pupils should learn:

- what to look for when describing physical features on the photograph
- to make use of precise geographical terminology
- to make use of descriptive writing or annotations.

Learning outcomes

By the end of this spread pupils should be able to:

- pinpoint major physical features by means of accurate arrows and annotations
- identify and describe the shape, size and perhaps colour of the physical features by the use of appropriate descriptive terms.

Key vocabulary

- key questions
- physical geography
- relief
- drainage

Skills builder

The skills involved and developed here will relate to the pupils' quality of written communication and the enhanced ability to describe and interpret the physical features on the photograph. They will develop the skill of being selective, by identifying only the major physical features which are important in giving the landscape its distinctiveness. It will help facilitate their skill of thinking geographically, by highlighting the physical feature by means of the appropriate geographic terms as well as using geographical descriptions and interpretations.

Further discussion activities

- How natural does the landscape shown on the photograph appear to be?
- Has the natural landscape been influenced by human actions at all?
- What have been the main agents responsible for making the landscape in the photograph look like it does today?

Answers to activities

1.
   - A 5 Mountain lake
   - B 6 Rough Grass
   - C 7 Coniferous woodland
   - D 4 Valley floor
   - E 2 Gentle slope
   - F 1 Steep Slope
   - G 3 Mountain summit
   - H 8 Patch of snow
   - I 9 Vertical cliffs
   - J 10 Scree

2. This part of Colorado is rugged and **mountainous**. The highest peaks are **pyramid**-shaped and have patches of **snow** on them. There are many **cliffs** and most of the land is very **rocky**. The main valley is **U-shaped** with smooth, steep sides. A small **lake** fills part of the valley floor.

   The higher mountains are **steep** and have little or no vegetation cover. The lower slopes are mainly covered in forest with some patches of rough **grass**.

3. The area around Tarn Hows is mountainous with the highest slopes covered in snow. Tarn Hows is situated in a broad, flat valley with most of the valley floor covered by the lake. The part of the valley floor not covered with water has grassland vegetation with a few scattered deciduous trees. There are also large areas of coniferous forest.

7 Key skills: writing and photos

Pupil Book pages 112–113

How can we use photographs to study settlements?

About this spread

This spread provides a checklist that pupils can use to describe aspects of settlement geography. It covers site and situation and the influence of physical and human factors in its development. Key geographical terms that should be used are emphasised. The pupils are shown how they can move from description of the features to an interpretation of their impact on a settlement's development.

Learning objectives

On this spread pupils should learn:

- that settlement patterns take many forms
- that both physical and human factors are important in understanding settlement geography
- to use appropriate geographical terminology when describing settlements on a photograph.

Learning outcomes

By the end of this spread pupils should be able to:

- know the difference between a settlement's site and its situation
- recognise different patterns of land use in settlements
- show that communications are important in the development of a settlement.

Key vocabulary

- settlement
- site
- land use

Skills builder

This spread will further extend the pupils' mastery of geographical terms and their use when applied to the shape, development and changes that are taking place within settlements. The opportunity should be made to use a photograph of a settlement with an OS map extract. Pupils should be able to name parts of the settlement and give the numbers of the main roads entering the settlement using the OS map.

Further discussion activities

- Which is the oldest part of a settlement and which is the newest?
- If new houses are to be built in the future where should they be built?
- What problems (traffic for example) is this settlement likely to be suffering from?
- Why will any modern development of Warkworth, shown on photograph C on page 49, be difficult?

Answers to activities

1.
   A 4 Car park
   B 7 Golf Course
   C 5 Housing estate
   D 3 Woodland
   E 1 Main road
   F 6 School
   G 8 Open countryside
   H 2 Town centre

2. Harlow is a new town in Essex. It is situated on **gently sloping** or **flat** land and spread out over a **large** area. There is plenty of open space and many **wooded areas** and parks. The town looks well **planned** and is neatly laid out. The **centre** has many tall buildings. Surrounding the centre are modern **housing estates** which all look very similar. An attractive, **landscaped** golf course is located on the **outskirts**. The town has a **good** network of main roads.

3. Ifracombe is situated in on the coast of Devon. Its site is at the head of bay overlooking a harbour. The town has now grown up the gentle slopes away from the sea. On either side of the town are areas that are too steep to build on, so these areas are left as bare rock or are covered in woodland. The town is quite compact, with the oldest part down by the sea and the more modern building inland on the slopes of the hills.

7 Key skills: writing and photos

Pupil Book pages 114–115

What do aerial photos show?

About this spread

On this spread pupils will learn what can be seen on vertical and oblique aerial photographs. They will recognise that aerial photographs can show features that are not possible to see on a map. An aerial photograph shows everything while a map has to be selective.

Learning outcomes

By the end of this spread pupils should be able to:

- use a map and an aerial photograph together to identify and possibly name locations or features
- recognise that unless the aerial photograph is a vertical one, it is not possible to measure distances from it, unlike on a map.

Key vocabulary

- aerial photos
- vertical air photos
- oblique air photos

Learning objectives

On this spread pupils should learn:

- that a map shows features differently – on a photograph they are shown as they actually are, but on a map they are represented by symbols
- that a map simplifies the detail but can add extra information such as names, which are not on the aerial photograph.

Skills builder

Pupils usually find oblique aerial photographs are easier to cope with, so as much practice as possible should be given for them to make use of vertical aerial photographs. Photographs should be used frequently with maps. Overlays can be used to identify and classify the different land uses or functions of the different parts of a settlement.

Further discussion activities

- What was the time of day/season of the year when the photograph was taken?
- What are the disadvantages of using an aerial photograph compared to a map?
- How could aerial photographs be useful for planners when considering the future growth of the town?

Answers to activities

1.
   a. Names of features and accurate distances.
   b. All features that are on the ground and a much larger area can be shown on a smaller piece of paper.

2.
   a.
      - A Blackbird Inn
      - B Allotments
      - C St Mary's Church
      - D Diamond Inn
      - E River Pont
      - F Greenhouses
      - G B6323
   b. The river is either in shadow or blocked out by trees.
   c. St Mary's Church

3.
   a.
      - A The O2 Arena
      - B An area of trees
      - C A roundabout
      - D A ship
      - E A main road
      - F A railway
      - G An industrial area
      - H An area of open space
      - I A smaller, tributary river
      - J An area of housing
   b. The river appears to be polluted because it is a dark green in colour and not transparent.

7 Key skills: writing and photos

Pupil Book pages 116–117

How can we use satellite photos?

About this spread

This spread introduces pupils to the potential of the use of satellite photos or images – photographs taken from space. It allows them to get an up-to-date picture of the earth and to appreciate the range of uses these images can be put to.

Learning objectives

On this spread pupils should learn:
- the nature of satellite images
- about the potential uses of satellite images by a wide range of interested parties.

Learning outcomes

By the end of this spread pupils should be able to:
- use a false colour key to identify features on a satellite image
- to name and locate features on a satellite image.

Key vocabulary

- **satellite photos or images**
- **false colours**

Skills builder

The use of satellite images will show pupils the potential of new developments in technology and how they give a much wider view of the world. This will contribute to the pupils' appreciation of the global dimension and their position as global citizens. The global approach will allow them to recognise that developments in one part of the world can impact internationally. The use of satellite imagery can contribute to pupils' understanding of sustainability.

Further discussion activities

- How might the use of satellite images help to understand the impact of global warming and other aspects of climate change?
- How widespread has been the deforestation of the tropical rain forests?
- What evidence is there that the world's deserts are getting larger?

Answers to activities

1. Fisherman – locate the best areas for fishing

   Farmer – assess insect damage or estimate crop yields

   Relief worker – assess the impact of a natural disaster such as flooding or a volcanic eruption

   Geologist – locate new mineral and oil resources

   Weather forecaster – predict weather patterns

   Surveyor – provide information for making maps

   Environmentalist – identify pollution problems such as oil spills

   Ship's captain – help ships avoid icebergs

2. False colours make some features stand out which would be difficult to see if natural colours were used.

3. **a** and **b**

   Note that the area to the north of the Golden Gate Bridge is indeterminate from the satellite image and the pupils may interpret it in different ways.

   c
   - (A) San Francisco Bay
   - (B) San Andreas Fault
   - (C) Montara Mountains
   - (D) Golden Gate Bridge
   - (E) San Francisco city centre
   - (F) Airport
   - (G) Golden Gate Park

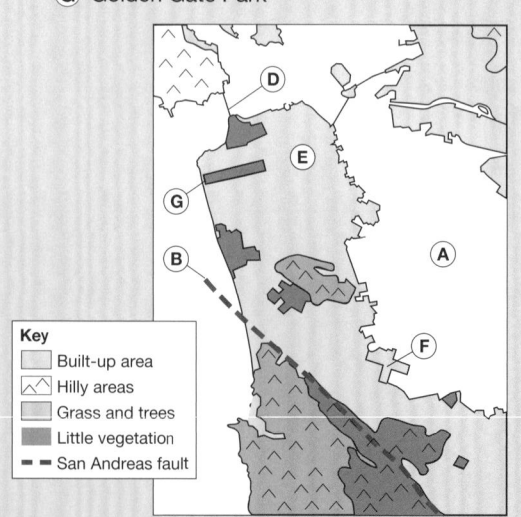

Appendix 1 — The weather enquiry

Section 1 — The Introduction

Have you: Student   Assessor
- included an aim
- defined the terms weather and climate
- included an annotated map that shows the regional pattern of weather in Britain
- described the different weather conditions found in the four climatic regions of Britain
- used facts and figures that highlight these differences?

Section 2 — To succeed make sure you:

Student   Assessor
- present accurate data in the table on page 30
- carry out detailed research to find accurate information on weather and climate
- colour code the table on page 30 to show patterns in the weather (hottest, wettest, coldest, driest)
- complete the tables for each family
- calculate the total points for each location to see which one suits best.

Section 3 — In your reply to the World Wide Leisure Corporation, include:

Student   Assessor
- four recommendations that match each family to a location in Britain
- reasons stating why this is the best location for each family
- specific facts and figures from the tables on page 31.

Extension — To really develop your answer:

Student   Assessor
- justify why the other sites were not suitable for each family.

Appendix 2 — The river flooding enquiry

Before you finish your enquiry use the reminders below to make sure that you have covered all of the correct points.

To make a well thought through and effective decision about the best flood protection scheme for the Doveton valley.

You will need to:	Student	Assessor
• make a copy of Table A on page 44 in the student book	☐	☐
• read the four scheme descriptions	☐	☐
• make a list of anything you are not sure about in the four scheme descriptions	☐	☐
• ask your teacher to explain the points you do not understand	☐	☐
• evaluate how successful each scheme would be by putting ticks in columns A, B, C, D of your table if the scheme would fulfil that factor	☐	☐
• add up the number of ticks for each scheme and write in the total score	☐	☐
• using the total score, make a decision about which scheme you would recommend	☐	☐
• think about which part of the valley you would like to protect most and then make your decision, if two schemes get the same total scores	☐	☐
• describe the scheme you would like to recommend	☐	☐
• justify your decision by explaining the benefits of your scheme for the Doveton valley	☐	☐
• state whether each of the four characters would be for or against your chosen scheme	☐	☐
• explain why each character would be for or against each scheme.	☐	☐

Appendix 3: The urbanisation enquiry

Before you finish your enquiry, use the reminders below to make sure you have covered all of the correct points.

Success criteria	A helpful resource	Self-evaluation	Teacher evaluation
1. Make sure your work is laid out like an official letter.			
2. Outline the problems that used to exist.	Analyse Figure A on page 71 in the student book.		
3. Describe the problems identified by your first environmental quality survey.	Activity 3b on page 70 in the student book.		
4. Make some recommendations about which of these problems you think is a priority to tackle first.	Look at Figures A and B on page 71. What if you could only make one change?		
5. Describe what can be done to improve the area.	Analyse Figure B on page 71 of the student book.		
6. Explain how you think the quality of the environment would change by using your results from the second survey.	Compare the results of your first environmental quality survey with the second you did. In which section of the survey did the score improve?		
7. Comment on your opinion.	Look carefully at both diagrams. Which do you prefer and why?		
8. List the other groups of people who you think would agree with you.	Use the people at the bottom of page 71 in the student book.		
9. Explain how these people would benefit.	Look carefully at Figure B on page 71 in the student book. How would life be easier for these people?		
10. Include a conclusion.			
11. Check your spelling and punctuation.			

Appendix 4 — The Kenya enquiry

Section 1: Calculating and comparing development

	Student
• Make a copy of table B on page 90 of the pupil book.	☐
• Use the information from diagram C on page 91 of the pupil book to complete the table.	☐
• Total the development score for each country.	☐
• Rank the order of development (the most developed will score 1).	☐
• Write out the countries as a 'league table of development'.	☐

Section 2: How developed is Kenya in comparison with the UK?

	Student	Peer
• Identify the differences between the UK and Kenya using information from table B on page 90 of the pupil book.	☐	☐
• Comment on any similarities.	☐	☐

Section 3: How developed is Kenya in comparison with its neighbouring countries in Africa

	Student	Peer	Assessor
• Identify the differences between neighbouring countries and Kenya using information from table B on page 90 of the pupil book.	☐	☐	☐

Section 4: Developing Kenya

	Student	Peer	Assessor
• Identify the areas in greatest need of development using the information from table B on page 90 of the pupil book.	☐	☐	☐
• Make at least one recommendation of what could be done to develop:			
– the wealth of the country (economically)	☐	☐	☐
– the standard of living and quality of life (socially)	☐	☐	☐
– the way of life (culturally).	☐	☐	☐

Extension

	Student	Peer	Assessor
• Justify each of your recommendations.	☐	☐	☐
• Be sure to refer to their suitability.	☐	☐	☐